Know You, Know Your Horse

An Intimate Look at Human and Horse Personalities

Identifying "Types" and Matchmaking to Ensure Long-Term Relationships

Eunice Rush & Marry Morrow

TRAFALGAR SQUARE
North Pomfret, Vermont

First published in 2012 by
Trafalgar Square Books
North Pomfret, Vermont 05053

Printed in China

Disclaimer of Liability
The authors and publisher shall have neither liability nor responsibility to any person or entity with respect to any loss or damage caused or alleged to be caused directly or indirectly by the information contained in this book. While the book is as accurate as the authors can make it, there may be errors, omissions, and inaccuracies.

While the horse and human relationship theories, techniques, and methods described in this book are drawn from the experience and knowledge of the authors, this book is not all-inclusive on the subject matter and may not apply in all circumstances. This book is intended to be an educational guideline only. When in doubt, readers should consult a professional. The human personality components included in this book are taken from a variety of experts and research. Neither author has a psychology background.

Trafalgar Square Books encourages the use of approved safety helmets in all equestrian sports.

Library of Congress Control Number: 2012955216

Book design by Lauryl Eddlemon
Cover design by RM Didier
Typefaces: Palatino, Myriad

10 9 8 7 6 5 4 3 2 1

Georganne –
Light of heart; living
life well!
you the best!
Marry Marrow

CAUTION!

READING THIS BOOK COULD BE DANGEROUS

UNLESS YOU ARE READY TO LOOK AT

YOURSELF, YOUR HORSE, AND YOUR

RELATIONSHIP WITH YOUR HORSE

IN A WHOLE NEW WAY.

Enjoy the journey
Eunice Rush

Contents

Glossary of Terms

As you prepare to navigate the pathway to personalities there are a few terms you need to understand.

LBI: Left Brain Introvert
LBE: Left Brain Extrovert
RBI: Right Brain Introvert
RBE: Right Brain Extrovert

Human Components

LEFT-BRAINED: Thought-based, logical. Better in math and science.
RIGHT-BRAINED: Emotion-based, creative. Better in music and arts.
INTROVERTED: Draws energy from within. Prefers quiet activities and being alone or with small groups.
EXTROVERTED: Draws energy externally. Enjoys being in large crowds. Is outgoing.

Human Core Personalities

ANALYST (LBI): Detailed, enjoys working alone.
POWERFUL (LBE): Goal focused, drives projects, and directs people.

MEDIATOR (LBI): Friendly, wants everyone to be happy.
ADVOCATE (RBE): Cheerleader type, outgoing, creative.

Horse Components

LEFT-BRAINED: Clever, playful, and willful. Good at new tasks. Likes a variety of jobs.
RIGHT-BRAINED: Alert, reactive and obedient. Prefers routine or familiar tasks.
INTROVERTED: Prefers to go slower, can do quick bursts of speed. Likes to be in the middle of a small group.
EXTROVERTED: Has more energy, endurance. Prefers long rides and moving his feet.

Horse Core Personalities

THINKER (LBI): Confident and "wants" to stand still.
WORKER (LBE): Confident and "wants" to move.
ACTOR (RBI): Fear-based and "needs" to stand still.
TALKER (RBE): Fear-based and "needs" to move.

"*Do you give the horse his strength or clothe his neck with a flowing mane? Do you make him leap like a locust, striking terror with his proud snorting? He paws fiercely, rejoicing in his strength, and charges into the fray. He laughs at fear, afraid of nothing; he does not shy away from the sword. The quiver rattles against his side, along with the flashing spear and lance. In frenzied excitement he eats up the ground; he cannot stand still when the trumpet sounds.*"

Job 39:19-25

Introduction

The Value of Knowing and Understanding Personality

I, Eunice, first met my co-author Marry as an attending student in one of her Frank Bell clinics. We seemed to just "hit if off" and soon became friends. One day while chatting about life in general we arrived at that age-related question, "So what did you do before you retired?"

As it turned out I had spent a lot of time coaching salespeople on how to read and align to clients. Marry had spent years reading the different horse personalities and aligning her personality and training methods accordingly. I started explaining to Marry how a human's personality is made up of distinctive and varying characteristics (traits) and that these are what make everybody act the way they do. So, when given the right approach and ability to read other people, you can "align" yourself with them and consequently, become more successful in personal relationships with family and friends; in business, sell your ideas and concepts as well as build effective teams; and use your knowledge to help in many other areas of life.

Marry then began to explain her theory about horses and how they also have distinctive personality traits; when you can recognize and "read" them you will be more successful in selecting and training your horse. So now we knew two things for sure:

- All people have a distinct core personality that embodies different behavioral characteristics and traits. Each person tends to respond better when interacting with some people rather than others.

- All horses also have a distinct core personality made up of several traits. Therefore, each horse also responds better when interacting with some people rather than others.

That's when the "light bulb" came on for me. "I wonder if there is any correlation to interactions between humans and the horses they love?" I did a quick analysis on Marry and we discussed her favorite horse of all time. We then did the same for me. Amazingly, the concept appeared true: riders and horses seemed happier with a partner who shared the same personality traits.

Of course we couldn't write a book based on an analysis of only two, so we started thinking about polling all our friends: I analyzed the person and Marry analyzed their favorite horse. Things just kept falling into place.

Next we came up some questionnaires that would help us analyze a bigger and unfamiliar group of people more quickly. The findings from the results were right on track with our theory. It appeared there really is a direct link between horse and rider because in most cases personality types were an exact match.

Unfortunately, we also discovered that many people found that "favorite" horse through much trial and error.

Finally, we went to various breeders and interviewed them (see chapter 9, p. 127). Here we found, more often than not, that the breeders who had been successful in placing horses seemed to have one thing in common: they were able to match a horse to a rider (and vice versa). When we asked how they did this we always got the same response: "I don't know how I know but I just know which horse is going to work for the customer." Interestingly, after they spent a day with us, our theory began to click for them too, and they began to understand how these matchups occurred: they had been subconsciously reading the people and matching their personalities to the correct horses.

Based on our findings, we believe horse and rider will be happier and more successful when both are in the correct relationship. We hope to enable *you* to understand the makeup of a human and of a horse and how the two fit together. Our goal through this knowledge, is to assist when you are:

- Looking to buy a great equine partner and need to know his traits in order to match your personalities or know if he is suitable for the riding discipline you want to pursue.

- Considering a horse to rescue that will benefit from your personality style.

- Wanting to look at each horse as a unique individual to customize your training accordingly. (This concept is moving away from the traditional way of thinking all horses should be trained using the same technique.)

- Trying to better understand the horse you have now.

In an attempt to keep the book both entertaining and yet educational, we've invented a group of horse owners and horses to demonstrate some core interactions. Most people or horses won't exactly match the characters depicted, but many of you will be able to say, "Yep, I'm a lot like that," or perhaps, "Yes, my horse sure does some of those things."

One very important point to make before we proceed is that there is no good and bad, or right and wrong when it comes to personalities. You are who you are. The horse is who he is. Every personality has a place in this world and each different personality has proven to be successful. The key is finding what works for each personality. When this happens, the horse or human may not only be successful, but also be happy doing it.

There is another key point we want to stress: this whole concept of having a different training method for each type of horse is unique—and contrary to the techniques used by many big-name trainers. Most trainers only have one approach and teach it in all their clinics; then you go home and repeat the process with your own horse. Some have even become "famous" for a particular type of training. Although we believe most good trainers have merit, we don't recommend any one in particular, but rather a combination of parts from all of their techniques. Overall, however, we are going to present a very different approach to training.

The book contains four main parts: The Human Personality; The Horse Personality; Matching Human to Horse and Horse to Human; and finally, Training Techniques for Your Horse's Social Style. Each section holds a piece of the overall puzzle but is designed so you can use what applies to you or delve deeper.

PART 1: THE HUMAN PERSONALITY

The first key element in matching horse and rider is identifying your core personality, known as your "Social Style." This section presents a brief overview of each human personality type, many charts, and appropriate tools of analysis, including a questionnaire to help you evaluate yourself.

PART 2: THE HORSE PERSONALITY

Once you have identified your core personality it is time to evaluate the horse. There are a series of descriptions and a questionnaire to assist you in this process. When you are just starting the search for a horse, you may need to ask his current owner to take the horse personality questionnaire.

PART 3: MATCHING HUMAN TO HORSE AND HORSE TO HUMAN

In addition to providing practical information on how to match up riders and horses and vice versa, this section gives you some examples of people working toward the purchase of their perfect horse. You will meet one of each of the human personality Social Styles depicted as a potential new horse owner. This is designed to give you a more in-depth understanding of each core personality. You will follow each person's quest through both perfect and not-so-perfect selections. We also explain how to choose suitable riding disciplines by horse personality type.

PART 4: TRAINING TECHNIQUES FOR YOUR HORSE'S SOCIAL STYLE

This section offers training methods with the horse's individuality in mind. A whole chapter is devoted to each of the four horse personality core Social Styles. The horse's traits: strengths and weaknesses, ability, and suitability to the various riding disciplines are discussed, along with training tips and techniques. Another chapter talks about the unique challenges of training a "rescue" horse.

PART ONE

The Human Personality

CHAPTER 1

Getting to
Know Yourself

W E KNOW YOU want to be told how you can quickly figure out what sort of "personality" you have. Well, if only it were that easy!

There are four different human personalities (also known as "Social Styles") that we'll describe in detail on the pages that follow, but for now you need to know that each of these "core" or basic personality styles is made up of different traits and characteristics common to that style. These traits (positive and negative) change as you go through life; however, you may well gain other traits as well as lose some.

The first type of change to your core personality occurs when you add traits usually associated with one or more of the other three core styles. As you mature, you do this subconsciously—to help balance your character. These additional traits are known as "modifiers"—tendencies that are almost always positive.

The second exception is twofold: first, change caused by a significant emotional event, which can alter your personality a great deal, even permanently. Also change caused by *temporary stress*, which alters your personality much less and probably temporarily. This means that you can totally change to a different (new) core personality style or change for the moment due to temporary stress (see the "Z" Pattern, p. 15).

The third type involves your job and whether you need to change your personality in order to keep it.

When your personality "changes" for whatever reason, unlike the horse you are still able to make logical decisions on how to react to any given situation. This ability to "alter" personality is how you are able to successfully align to other humans (and horses) on a case-by-case basis, for example, to promote an idea (and train a horse).

The Four Basic Social Styles

In this chapter, I am going to introduce the basic different types of human personality—the *four* Social Styles. These are:

1 **Analyst**
Focus: Finding facts
Brief description: Is good at strategizing and organization.
Typically says: "How?"
(For an in-depth discussion of the *Analyst,* see p. 58.)

2 **Powerful**
Focus: Achieving goals
Brief description: Gets the job done, achieves.
Typically says: "What?"
(For an in-depth discussion of the *Powerful,* see p. 61.)

3 **Mediator**
Focus: Relationships

Brief description: Is good at communication and teamwork.

Typically says: "Who?"

(For in-depth discussion of the *Mediator,* see p. 64.)

4 **Advocate**

Focus: Creativity

Brief description: Is conceptual, theoretical, innovative

Typically says: "Why?"

(For in-depth discussion of the *Advocate*, see p. 67.)

See the chart on p. 12 for a brief overview of the traits associated with these four Social Styles (fig. 1.1).

Each of these four core Social Styles is comprised of traits that evolve from four components listed below. (For an in-depth look at these components, see pp. 33 to 37). The two most influential are *Left/Right Brain,* and *Introvert/Extrovert*. When put all together, these four components produce the personality traits that are responsible for establishing your core Social Style. The components are:

- Left Brain / Right Brain
- Introvert / Extrovert
- Birth Order
- Learning Method

To learn about the specific traits associated with each of these components, see the chart on p. 12.

Understanding your social style and modifiers—strengths, preferences and weaknesses—helps you to become a more balanced person by focusing on your strengths and modifying your weaknesses. Through this knowledge, you may also decide to work differently, interact differently with people, or surround yourself with people possessing complementary strengths.

Common Social Style Traits

The chart below contains a *brief* summary of a human's most common traits associated with each Social Style. (More complete lists of the traits attributed to all four Social Styles are presented in chapter 4: *Analyst*, p. 58; *Powerful*, p. 61; *Mediator,* p. 64; *Advocate*, p. 67.)

ANALYST	POWERFUL	MEDIATOR	ADVOCATE
Process-Driven (Left Brain Introvert—LBI)	Action-Driven (Left Brain Extrovert—LBE)	People-Driven (Right Brain Introvert—RBI)	Idea-Driven (Right Brain Extrovert—RBE)
Pensive	Impatient	Accommodating	Overly enthusiastic
Logical	Quick	Friendly	Dramatic
Detailed	Abrupt	Compliant	Motivates
Methodical	Goal-oriented	Subservient	Artsy
Rational	Assertive	Good planner	Creative
Quiet	Self-confident	Loyal	Loud
Analyzes to death	Doesn't like detail	Enjoys being part of the team	Cheerleader with "team" sense
Conducts own research and asks a lot of questions	Driven; tells people what to do	Has trouble saying "no"	Has high energy
Has trouble making decisions	Makes decisions quickly	Has trouble making decisions	Makes decisions quickly
Good at making master schedules	Good at defining new concepts	Good at keeping the team working together	Good at seeing the big picture
Will ask you what you think	Will tell you what you should think	Will ask you how you feel	Will tell you how you should feel

1.1

THE SOCIAL STYLE GRID

While no one likes to be put in boxes, that is, in effect, what your core personality style does for you. Imagine a big box divided equally into four parts. Give each part the name of a Social Style appearing from top left to bottom right in this order: *Analyst; Powerful, Mediator* and *Advocate* (fig. 1.2). Now add to these Social Styles the Left/Right Brain and Extrovert/Introvert components

The Social Style Grid

ANALYST	POWERFUL
Left Brain (Thoughtful and Logical)	Left Brain (Thoughtful and Logical)
Introvert (Asks)	Extrovert (Tells)
MEDIATOR	ADVOCATE
Right Brain (Emotional and Creative)	Right Brain (Emotional and Creative)
Introvert (Asks)	Extrovert (Tells)

1.2

that match them: People in the *top* half of the grid are "thinkers" (thoughtful/logical) and in the *bottom* half are "feelers" (emotional/creative). The *left* half contains "introverts" and the *right* half includes the "extroverts."

PERSONALITY MODIFIERS

In order to determine your core personality from the questionnaire (Social Styles evaluator) coming up in the next chapter, you will need to determine into which quadrant of the grid the majority of your traits fall. For example, let's say the majority of your traits are those of a Left Brain Extrovert: this makes your core Social Style a *Powerful.* Other traits that are not associated with a *Powerful* will come from at least one, if not all, of the other three core personality styles; these are the traits we call *personality modifiers* (tendencies). So if your second highest score is made up of Left Brain Introvert traits, your primary modifier will be *Analyst,* and you are known as a *Powerful/Analyst.*

THE BALANCED (OR UNBALANCED) INDIVIDUAL

While there are no good or bad, and right or wrong Social Styles, the traits that make up each personality style can be *positive* or *negative*. In order to become a more balanced person, the key is to identify all your traits and work to eliminate the negative ones and replace them with positive ones. As you mature, you will tend to naturally select or add traits that help you to be more successful in life. Therefore, most of the traits you use from your Social Style *modifiers* will tend to be the positive ones.

As you become more balanced, the better you will be able to align with people and horses from all core Social Styles. Somebody who has an equal number of traits from all four quadrants—that is, is very balanced—is certainly the exception but a person you can work toward emulating.

At the other end of the scale, there are people who have traits from only one of the four Social Styles. Without any modifiers from other Social Styles they will display both the positive and the negative traits associated with that Style: for example, a *Mediator* might have the subservient trait; an *Analyst*, lacking common sense; a *Powerful* could be pushy; and an *Advocate*, loud.

CHANGING YOUR CORE STYLE

As I mentioned earlier, a person's Social Style may alter as a result of stress. Sometimes this can have long-lasting effects, while other times only for the short term. Social Style can also be altered because of the influence of a job.

First, an item that can temporarily alter your core Social Style is the function of work where you assume the traits needed to do your job. In addition to the fact that your job can alter your personality to some degree and cause you to misjudge your own Social Style, it is particularly important you understand its influence when you take the Social Styles Questionnaire on page 21.

You need to determine if your job reflects your Social Style or vice versa.

Some people are lucky enough to find a job that fits perfectly. Others are not so lucky. An example is the *Advocate* who works in advertising. This is a perfect match because an *Advocate* is creative and outgoing. Her scores will not be impacted by her job. However, when a *Mediator* suddenly ends up as supervisor at work and has to tell people what to do, she will likely do it to keep her job. She won't like it. It will probably cause her stress at work, and if someone were to ask her about her personality she might well say "I tell people what to do" even though that is not a core trait of a *Mediator.* She would need to take time to think back to her core values, particularly when not at work, and certainly when she takes the questionnaire on p. 21.

The "Z" Pattern

Second, another type of change is when you face everyday types of stress. In this case you might find your core Social Style is altered, but when that immediate stress is over, you go right back to your original personality. When this type of short-term change occurs, you are forced to "cross the boundary lines" of the Social Styles grid in the "Z" pattern. It is called this because as you go through each step of the process, the line you take forms a "Z" on the grid (see the example of an *Analyst* in figs. 1.3 A & B).

The reason a person crosses the boundary lines in the grid in a "Z" pattern is because it is always easier for her to first move to a Social Style that shares her same left or right brain component. For example, when an *Analyst* becomes stressed she will first move to *Powerful* (the next style on the grid and the one that shares the left brain). If the stress continues she can move on to *Mediator* and, finally, even to *Advocate*—both right brain styles. However, as soon as the stress subsides, she will return to being an *Analyst*.

Finally, when you have to deal with a significant emotional event such as a death, divorce, or a major move, you might incur a personality change that lasts for a long time. With this type of long-lasting change, your core personality can be altered to a Style from any of the other three quadrants.

Analyst "Z" Pattern

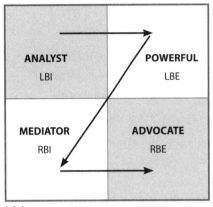

1.3 A

Mediator "Z" Pattern

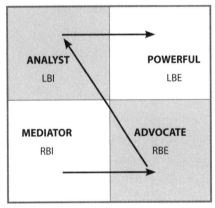

1.3 B

This is because your level of stress dictates where you stop the "Z" pattern. For example an *Analyst* might "Z" to a *Powerful* and then be able to handle the stress at that level. In that case she will not stress further. Where you end up depends on what you need to do to survive the event.

ALIGNING TO OTHERS

While it is important to understand your own Social Style, it is equally important to understand another person's style when dealing with her in matters of importance. You must determine her Social Style, then temporarily "alter" (or adjust) your own Social Style to match hers. This is called "aligning." It is a process in which you make her more comfortable.

You need to be very flexible: a good salesperson is a master at this skill (this will come in useful when selling a horse!). In this situation, you must first identify the other person's Social Style and then quickly align. You have about 60 seconds. Ask yourself a few quick questions. Does she use the word "think" or "feel" when she talks? A right-brained person will generally say "feel" and other similar words. A left-brained person generally says "think" and associated thought-based words.

Does she seem to be "asking" you questions or "telling" you information? An Introvert usually "asks," while an Extrovert most likely "tells."

Once you have identified the Social Style, align to it by using the actions shown in fig. 1.4.

Sharing a similar Social Style builds comfort and trust between people. But, should you make a mistake and misjudge the other person, you may start to notice her personality start to change. This is the beginning of her "Z" pattern kicking in because, as you have surely experienced in life, it can often become a bit uncomfortable interacting with someone who has a different personality from yours.

For example, let's say you are trying to sell a horse to a *Mediator* and have misjudged her to be a *Powerful*. You have jumped right in with the high-level

How to Align with Others

AN ANALYST	A POWERFUL
• Have your facts straight • Be prepared to answer and ask questions • Don't jump around topics • Be logical • Pay close attention to humor • Be patient • Don't expect quick decisions • Make suggestions	• Have your facts straight but don't use them unless they are solicited • Get to the point • Don't waste time • Be prompt • Don't ask too many detailed questions

A MEDIATOR	AN ADVOCATE
• Be nice • Indulge digressions • Be patient • Lead the discussion • Make suggestions • Initiate pleasant conversation • Smile a lot • Nod a lot	• Be enthusiastic • Indulge digressions • Have some fun trivia to share • Be eclectic • Pay attention • Champion a cause • Compliment

1.4

details and sales pitch. The *Mediator* will start out caring and friendly but when you don't return her small talk, she may show hurt feelings, stop asking questions and even become a bit aggressive. This is the start of the "Z" pattern where a *Mediator* first becomes an *Advocate*: She is moving from the introverted trait of "asking" to the extroverted trait of "telling." When you realize your mistake, adjust your approach and observe her reaction. If she returns to the friendly, feeling, questioning person, you have now guessed her core style and adjusted yours correctly.

Another critical reason to become a "flexible" person in the matter of Social Styles is for training horses, or doing any work around a "rescue" horse, or one that has been abused. A good trainer "reads" the horse and aligns her personality with his.

While you may only have 60 seconds for aligning to a person, you can take as much time as you need with a horse as long as you don't start the training process until you know. So invest the time to first make the necessary observations. This will be discussed in detail in Part Two: The Horse Personality.

Summary

Regardless of your Social Style, you will be more successful in relationships when you learn to recognize various different personalities and understand how to align case by case. As you will learn later, this is critical when training horses.

Being able to be "flexible" is a skill everyone should develop for the comfort of other people you come into contact with. However, when you are looking for that long-lasting relationship—with another person or a horse—you should find a partner who does not require you to change your core personality, and that means a partner whose Social Style matches yours.

The Human Foundation

In general, left-brained people are more logical, while right-brained people are more creative. Introverts take more time to make decisions, are more detailed, quiet, and enjoy spending time alone. Extroverts make decisions quickly, are more energetic and are very outgoing. The table below lists the human qualities associated with these components.

LEFT BRAIN (Analyst & Powerful) "Thinks"	RIGHT BRAIN (Mediator & Advocate) "Emotes"	INTROVERT (Analyst & Mediator) "Asks"	EXTROVERT (Powerful & Advocate) "Tells"
Logical	Philosophical	Quiet	Outgoing
Rational	Feeling	Draws energy from within	Draws energy from the people around her
Organized	Random	Reserved	Assertive
Detailed	Intuitive	Forms deep, close friendships	Has several surface level friendships
Good at science and/or math	Good at arts and/or creativity	Prefers to be alone or with one or two close friends	Enjoys large groups of acquaintances
Objective: Makes decisions based on analyzing facts	Subjective: Makes decisions on personal views and opinions	Problem-solver	Motivator
Makes lists and checks them off	Looks at "whole" then works to "parts"	Good at remembering events	Tuned in to environment
Does tasks in order	Often flits from one task to the next	Is good at organizing events	Works best in groups
Follows directions easily	Flexible and can change direction easily	Low-keyed	Enthusiastic
Good with symbols	Has trouble finding correct words to express herself	Good at organizing	Good at giving presentations
Wants to know the rules	Day dreams	Private	Easy to get to know
Follows the rules	Needs to feel, see, taste, smell	Has trouble sharing feelings	Open with feelings
Makes master schedules	Does tasks randomly	Is a loyal friend	Enjoys sensory events
Works from "parts" to "whole"	Sees the whole picture then adds the parts	Is reserved in large groups	Naturally responsive with people
Gives directions in compass points and miles	Uses landmarks when giving directions	Good at remembering events	Quick wit
Good communicator	Good teacher	More productive in quiet settings	More productive in high energy settings
Persuasive	Needs to see the word in context when learning	Concerned about what people think about them	Self-confident
Uses the word "think"	Uses the word "feel"	Does more "asking"	Does more "telling"

CHAPTER 2

The Social Style
Questionnaire

WHEN YOU TAKE this questionnaire in order to establish your Social Style, it is important that you understand these various types of shifts in core personality that I discussed in the last chapter because you will need to align your personality to a horse based on your *core* Social Style, not an "altered" version. This means you should do the questionnaire when you are at your most comfortable, that is, relaxed and rested and not stressed by events or influenced by your job's requirements.

Each question asks you to pick one of two statements. There will be some questions where you think both statements describe you. In these cases, pick the one you *value* the most. For example, take questions 49 and 50 where you need to decide between choosing: "I inquire about other people's lives," or "I enjoy doing different things." You should choose which one of these is more important to you.

Follow these directions carefully:

1 Come up with your answer quickly and don't try to second guess it.

2 Don't base it on what you think "should" be the right answer. For example, Number 61 says "People think I am a visionary," and Number 62 states, "People say I am good with details." If your friends value visionaries you might be tempted to select 61 when, actually, 62 describes you much better.

3 As mentioned earlier, you must try to keep your daily job skills from affecting your answers in the questionnaire because these can taint the results. These skills, whether mathematical or organizational, for example, may influence your core Social Style—depending on your traits and the job, of course.

4 Answer honestly. Honesty is critical when you take any of the questionnaires but especially this one.

Evaluating Your Social Style

To evaluate your Social Style, select *one* item from each of the 40 pairs of statements by choosing which of the traits best describes you, as well as reflects what you value as an important quality. You have options as to how you determine your score: circle each chosen item's number, or photocopy the page; jot it down on a separate piece of paper; or download the questionnaire from the *Know You, Know Your Horse* book page on the Trafalgar Square Books website (www.horseandriderbooks.com). You should have 40 items marked at the conclusion of the exercise. (Remember there is no *wrong* answer.)

1. I like to be doing things.
2. I manage problems in an orderly way.

---

3. I like change.
4. I think teams are more productive than individuals.

---

5. I prefer working with people.
6. The future interests me more than the past.

---

7. I prefer the practical.
8. I enjoy a well-organized meeting.

---

9. It is best to get things done now.
10. I test new ideas thoroughly before using them.

---

11. I enjoy trying to think of new possibilities.
12. Interaction with others is a high priority.

---

13. I can easily take charge in a project.
14. I like to take one thing at a time through to the end.

---

15. I often stimulate people to think.
16. I can often detect what people are feeling.

---

17. Getting feedback to improve performance is important.
18. A step-by-step approach is best to solve problems.

---

19. I can sense the emotion beneath the surface.
20. I can find creative solutions.

21. Thinking about the future is enjoyable for me.
22. Meeting other people's needs is enjoyable.

---

23. Success depends upon good planning.
24. I am more action than talk.

---

25. Under pressure I tend to analyze.
26. I learn best through experience.

---

27. People think I am a good listener.
28. People say I am a creative thinker.

---

29. I am prone to procrastination.
30. I am logical and thorough.

---

31. I am always looking for a better way.
32. I can handle several tasks at the same time.

---

33. I can make quick decisions.
34. I follow my head more than my heart.

---

35. I like seeing the bigger picture.
36. It is best to talk-out your problems.

---

37. Thinking should always precede action.
38. I am good at encouraging others.

---

39. I accomplish more by working alone.
40. I like to start things and let others finish them.

---

41. I enjoy taking on new tasks.
42. I think that facts speak for themselves.

43. I am in touch with my feelings.
44. I seek to know "why."
_____

45. I prefer reading the thoughts of others.
46. I perceive myself as a helper.
_____

47. I do one thing at a time and do it well.
48. I get the job done and don't look back.
_____

49. I inquire about other people's lives.
50. I enjoy doing different things.
_____

51. If you are going to do it, do it right.
52. Be creative and stretch your mind.
_____

53. I am impatient with incompetent people.
54. My mind works fast.
_____

55. I minimize risk by moving slowly.
56. Working cooperatively is more impor-
    tant than working efficiently.
_____

57. I can adjust to circumstances.
58. Feelings are not as trustworthy as facts.
_____

59. Being liked is important to me.
60. I usually grasp an idea very quickly.
_____

61. People think I am a visionary.
62. People say I am good with details.

63. I prefer productivity/accomplishments.
64. Good relationships are essential.
_____

65. I am quick to take on new jobs.
66. I take the initiative to make new people
    feel comfortable.
_____

67. I often think about the purpose of life.
68. I really enjoy selecting just the right
    greeting card for others.
_____

69. Organizing is one of my strengths.
70. Getting things done is my strength.
_____

71. Finding meaning is important to me.
72. Working together is better than
    just working.
_____

73. I play with ideas even if they are
    impractical.
74. I believe rules are made to be followed.
_____

75. Quality is to be preferred over quantity.
76. I learn better in groups.
_____

77. I make decisions in a methodical way.
78. I like ideals and tend to be idealistic.
_____

79. I say what I mean and mean what I say.
80. I am very accepting of others.

SCORING

Got your answers? Now you can score them.

1 You should now have 40 numbers picked from the questionnaire. Locate the numbers listed under each of the four Social Styles headings below. The Social Style under which the *majority* of your chosen numbers appear will reveal your *core Social Style*. The next highest score indicates the Social Style that is your *primary modifier*, followed by your *secondary modifier*, and so on. (Remember, nearly everyone has at least one personality *modifier* and, in fact, most will pick a few answers from every category.)

2 Add up your total score of Left Brain and Right Brain answers (*Analysts* and *Powerfuls* are left-brained; *Mediators* and *Advocates* are right-brained).

3 Also add up your total score of Introvert and Extrovert answers (*Analysts* and *Mediators* are Introverts; *Powerfuls* and *Advocates* are Extroverts).

Style 1—ANALYST
Left Brain Introvert *(LBI)*
Answers: 2, 8, 10, 14, 18, 23, 25, 30, 34, 37, 42, 47, 51, 55, 58, 62, 66, 69, 75, 77

Style 2—POWERFUL
Left Brain Extrovert *(LBE)*
Answers: 1, 7, 9, 13, 17, 24, 26, 32, 33, 39, 41, 48, 50, 53, 57, 63, 65, 70, 74, 79

Style 3—MEDIATOR
Right Brain Introvert *(RBI)*
Answers: 4, 5, 12, 16, 19, 22, 27, 29, 36, 38, 43, 46, 49, 56, 59, 64, 68, 72, 76, 80

Style 4—ADVOCATE

Right Brain Extrovert *(RBE)*

Answers: 3, 6, 11, 15, 20, 21, 28, 31, 35, 40, 44, 45, 52, 54, 60, 61, 67, 71, 73, 78

In order to explain how the scoring works let's look at Terry.

Terry

Terry's questionnaire scores are *Analyst* 4; *Powerful* 8; *Mediator* 18; *Advocate* 10. *Left Brain* 12; *Right Brain* 28. *Introvert* 22; *Extrovert* 18.

What do these numbers say about Terry?

Terry is definitely a *Mediator* and her *primary modifier* is an *Advocate*. She is probably one of the nicest people you would ever want to meet. When her friends need an event, she is there to help because she is good at organizing a party. She enjoys remembering everyone's birthday and getting them "the" special card but sometimes it takes a while because she has problems making decisions quickly.

She is so high scoring in her core style, she may well be one of those people who can't say no; consequently, she is taken advantage of at times. The good news is that she is high enough in the *Advocate* area so she can likely stand up for herself.

Mediators love small talk and keeping everyone happy. She always remembers to ask about people's family and important events in their lives. She can be good at music and art.

Her *Advocate* side can make her good at theater and interior design or fashion. Her *Powerful* traits, however, make her uncomfortable because they can cause her to start telling others what to do—somewhat of a conflict for a *Mediator*.

The *Analyst* traits provide her lowest score but "good at detail" characteristics are present because she enjoys pulling together a project. Terry will be good at the detailed planning for a party or event and its implementation, but because both *Mediators* and *Analysts* have trouble making decisions quickly, she will need a *Powerful* or *Advocate* at her side for final decisions.

She has 28 Right Brain and 12 Left Brain answers so is definitely more emotion-driven than logical. (And because she is higher in the Introvert column—22 vs. 18 for Extrovert—we recommend an Introvert horse. See p. 75 for horse analysis.)

For further clarification, here are some more examples:

Brenda

Brenda scored as follows: *Analyst* 10; *Powerful* 12; *Mediator* 4; *Advocate* 14. *Left Brain* 22; *Right Brain* 18; *Introvert* 14; *Extrovert* 26.

What does this say about her?

Brenda's top three Social Styles scores are quite close. Her highest of 14 reveals *Advocate* as her core Style. As an *Advocate*, her profile is a cheerleader type; she enjoys big crowds; uses big hand and body movements; is probably good with fashion design and/or theater; has very high energy; may be self-centered; has no regard for time schedules; doesn't care for details (unless it is something of importance to her); and makes decisions quickly (usually based on emotion).

Her next highest score is *Powerful,* her primary modifier. This is interesting because an *Advocate* is *right-brained* while a *Powerful* is *left-brained*. We would assume Brenda is emotion-based since she is first an *Advocate*, but when you look at her numbers you see that it is her Extrovert high score that primarily qualifies her as an *Advocate*. And because she actually scores higher under Left Brain, more of the traits she picks up from *Powerful* will likely be logical attributes. Therefore, she will likely make decisions based on logic; be great at directing other people's activities; and be goal-oriented. (However, either way, she is probably a great presenter because both *Advocates* and *Powerfuls* have this Extrovert trait.)

The other possible conflicts here are that *Powerfuls* are always on time, and want to know and follow the rules while *Advocates* usually don't.

Her third highest score is *Analyst,* which isn't surprising because her left-brained score is 22 compared to her 18 for the right brain. Consequently, as mentioned, being more left-brained Brenda probably reacts logically more often than emotionally. However, *Analysts* like detail, while *Powerfuls* and *Advocates* generally don't, so I doubt she would enjoy this sort of work. *Analysts* are Introverts and enjoy a quiet time alone or with two or three close friends. However, since Brenda's Introvert score is so much lower than her Extrovert score (14 vs. 26) this probably isn't the case for Brenda.

Finally, the *Mediator* comes in with only 4 points. This fits well with the fact that she has 26 Extrovert points. Extroverts are very comfortable telling people what to do, while *Mediators* tend to want everyone to be happy and are uncomfortable as leader. Brenda probably has few, or no traits from this Social Style.

Because it is quite uncommon to have nearly equal scores in both left and right brain Brenda might want to do a final clarification by asking herself a couple of questions:

"Was I under any unusual stress when I answered the questionnaire?" The reason for this question is because her scores indicate a perfect "Z" pattern (p. 15). If she answers yes, then her results could have been affected. She might, in fact, be a much stronger *Advocate*, stressing through the "Z" pattern to *Analyst;* or she could be a *Powerful* stressing toward *Mediator*.

"Does my job require me to be an *Analyst* or *Powerful*?" If so, she should look at the list of traits for these personalities and try to determine if she thinks she fits one list more than the other.

If the answer to both of these questions is "No," then the description of her outlined on p. 28 will be pretty accurate. Her Extrovert score is 26, Introvert is 14. Therefore, Brenda will do better with an Extrovert horse.

Tom

When Tom took his questionnaire he scored the following: **Powerful** 11, **Analyst** 15, **Mediator** 9, and **Advocate** 5; **Left Brain** 26; **Right Brain** 14; **Introvert** 24; **Extrovert** 16.

Tom is very much an **Analyst** type with a score of 15. He is good with details, likes to get in and dig for information on his own, works well alone, prefers one or two really close friends, likes quiet times, is logical and good in math and science.

Next is **Powerful** with a score of 11. **Powerfuls** are also left-brained, but Extroverts. Tom might be a technical type who has been promoted to a leadership position. If so, his job would require him to direct projects and employees. This would cause him to score high as a **Powerful**. Or, it could just be his core nature to also be goal-focused, driven, be able to direct people, converse, and present information well.

Then comes **Mediator** with a score of 9. Like his core Style, **Analyst,** the **Mediator** is also an Introvert, but emotion-based (right-brained). Tom can be someone who wants people to be happy, is one of the really good guys, enjoys small talk and is creative—maybe music or art.

Finally, he has a 5 in **Advocate**. This can also link to the **Powerful** part in that he might enjoy teaching a night class somewhere, or maybe playing in a band or displaying his art.

Tom's total score indicates he is 26 Left Brain and 14 Right Brain, more logical than emotion driven. Because he scored higher as an Introvert (24 vs.16 for Extrovert), he will likely do well with an Introvert horse.

Ben

Ben's questionnaire scores are: *Analyst* 10, *Powerful* 10, *Mediator* 10, and *Advocate* 10; *Left Brain* 20; *Right Brain* 20; *Introvert* 20; *Extrovert* 20.

What does this tell us about Ben?

Ben is either a totally balanced person or he is totally stressed, either in general or when just taking the questionnaire. There are four reasons Ben could have scored this way:

- He is stressed.
- His job requires him to regularly assume non-core traits.
- He analyzed the questionnaire questions before answering them.
- He is a balanced person.

Assuming these results are not caused by stress, his job, or the way he took the test, Ben is the kind of person who can get along with just about any person and do well at many types of jobs. To really understand Ben you would need to look at the list of traits in every Social Style category and have him pick the ones that fit his personality. Only then could you know his core personality traits. Ben has probably learned over time to develop the traits that have allowed him to be successful and eliminate those that don't. He could have had several significant emotional events in his life that have caused him to reside in each of the personality quadrants for a period of time. During each phase of his life he has taken with him the traits he enjoyed.

Ben's total score indicates he is 20 Left Brain and 20 Right Brain, equally logical and emotion driven. Because he scored equally as an Introvert and Extrovert, he will likely do well with any horse or discipline that interests him.

· · · · · · · · · ·

Your Social Style is made up from the various traits associated with four basic human components. It is the combination of these components' traits that defines your personality whether *Analyst; Powerful; Mediator;* or *Advocate.* A reminder that the four components are:

- Right Brain/Left Brain
- Introvert/Extrovert
- Birth Order
- Learning Style

They will be discussed in detail in the next chapter.

CHAPTER 3

The Four Components That Define Human Personality

Left or Right Brain?

Experimentation has shown that the two different sides, or hemispheres, of the brain are responsible for different manners of thinking. *Analysts* and *Powerfuls* are *left-brained* (thought/logic-based) people while *Mediators* and *Advocates* are *right-brained* (emotion/creative-based).

Statistically speaking, men are more left-brained and women more right-brained. Additionally, society typically "treats" males as left-brained and females as right-brained. If this theory is enforced enough during our formative years, it can modify our core behavior and Social Style. Birth order also seems to have some influence on the core personality in young children. (For more on birth order, see p. 39.) The table in fig. 3.1 illustrates the differences between left- and right-brained thinking.

Differences Between Left and Right Brain

LEFT BRAIN (thought-based)	RIGHT BRAIN (emotion-based)
• Logical • Sequential • Rational • Analytical • Objective • Looks at "parts"	• Creative • Random • Intuitive • Subjective • Looks at the "whole"

3.1

You will often see left-brained people referred to as logical or thought-based, while right-brained people are described as creative or emotion-based. The thought-based person's brain controls verbal ability, attention to detail, and reasoning. She is good at communication and persuading others.

If you are *thought-based,* you are probably good at math and logic. You enjoy dogs, reading, and quiet times. You have a hard time visualizing abstracts. For example, a right-brained person can often look at a room and imagine what it would look like if decorated differently. The left-brained person has to see a picture of it.

If you are *emotion-based,* your brain is all about creativity and flexibility. You are likely intuitive and have a talent for creative writing, art, decorating, and fashion. You enjoy day dreaming, philosophy, and sports. You struggle with math and science and things that you have to do in steps.

Most individuals distinctly prefer one of these styles of thinking. Some, however, are more "whole-brained" and are equally adept at both modes. This also leads to being a more balanced Social Style person.

A thought-based person's brain processes information in a linear manner.

It processes from part to whole: taking pieces, lining them up, and arranging them in a logical order and then drawing conclusions. You might find the left-brained person putting together a list of pros and cons to do an evaluation of some product or event. This person has no problem writing a paper piece by piece and then putting it all together.

Emotion-based people however, process from the whole to parts. Unless given the big picture first, right-brained people may have difficulty following a lecture. This is why it is always good to follow the old rule of presenting, "Tell them what you are going to tell them, tell them, and then tell them what you told them." This person needs to know what the paper is going to look like when it is completed, then builds sections to make them fit the whole.

If you are thought-based, you enjoy making master schedules and daily planning. You complete tasks in order and take pleasure in checking them off the list when they are accomplished. By contrast, the emotion-based person does things in a more random fashion. You may flit from one task to another. You will get just as many tasks completed, but perhaps without having addressed the real priorities.

Left-brained people tend to be comfortable with linguistic and mathematical endeavors. They want everything to be concrete. On the other hand, the right-brained are happy if they can memorize the vocabulary and some math formulas. Left-brained people love to do math games and puzzles—ones with an exact answer. You will rarely find a right-brained person doing these—she's more likely to enjoy crafts that are hands-on and creative.

A thought-based person uses information piece by piece to solve a math problem or work out a science experiment. When she reads and listens, she looks for the "pieces" so she can draw logical conclusions. However, if she "processes" primarily as emotion-based, she uses intuition. She may know the correct answer to a math problem but not be exactly sure how she got it.

The right side of the brain pays attention to coherence and meaning—that is, it tells her if it "feels" right. A quick key to knowing if you or someone else may be right-brained or left-brained is by the words used in everyday speech. The right-brained person will tend to use "feeling" words, for example, "That just doesn't *feel* right to me." The left-brained person will use "thought" words such as, "I just don't *think* that is right."

"Thought" people have little trouble expressing themselves in words. Emotive people may know what they mean, but often have trouble finding the right words. The best illustration of this is to listen to the way people give directions. The left-brained person will say something like, "From here, go West three blocks and turn North on Vine Street. Go three or four miles and then turn East onto Broad Street." The right-brained person will give the directions like this: "Turn right (pointing right), by the church over there (pointing again). Then, you will pass a McDonalds and a Wal-Mart. At the next light, turn right toward the BP station."

Thought-based people deal with things "just the way they are," that is, with "reality." When they are affected by what is going on around them—traffic jams or family bickering, for example—they usually adjust easily. Not so with emotion-based (right-brained) people. They try to change the environment to fit them so they feel more comfortable. The thought-based want to know the rules and will follow them, while the emotion-based are sometimes not even aware what the rules are—or even that there are any rules. So, if you are the latter, make sure you constantly ask for feedback and reality checks from others.

The emotional student is creative. She will be much better in art class than the logical student. However, music can go either way. There is a lot of logic in the creation of music. However, the right-brained are more likely to "play by ear."

The logic-based, left-brained person might have a problem with a fear-based, right-brained horse, and vice versa. When the person needs to sit and process a thought but her horse first needs to "get out of Dodge" and *then* think, the differences between them might not work—for rider or horse.

When deciding on a job it is always better for everyone involved if you can find one that suits your brain. For example, a left-brained person might be more comfortable and more successful as a computer programmer. And, just like people, horses do certain jobs (different disciplines) better when their personality matches what you want them to do. For example, introverted horses are better at dressage than Extroverts (see p. 89).

Introvert or Extrovert?

The second component that helps to make up your Social Style is *Introvert* or *Extrovert*. **Analysts** and **Mediators** are Introverts, while **Powerfuls** and **Advocates** are Extroverts. As a general description, an Introvert is a person who is reserved, quiet, and solitary; an Extrovert is a person who is outgoing, assertive, and social.

More specifically, an Introvert is more concerned with and interested in her own thoughts than those of the external world. Introverts are often seen as shy and prefer to spend time on their own or with one or two close friends. When alone, the Introvert feels more energized and can work more productively.

On the other hand, an Extrovert is more focused on external things such as other people and situations. An Extrovert may feel bored when she is alone and can usually accomplish more when working in a group, where she is very comfortable.

Extroverts may be even happier when the center of attention. This is especially true of the **Advocate**. Traditional Extrovert personality traits are self-confident, enthusiastic, gregarious, friendly, and outgoing. They love crowds, public demonstrations, community events, and other large social gatherings: The more people around, the better life is! A significant extroverted personality trait is that energy flows *outward* (not *inward*—as happens with the Introvert). Extroverts like **Powerfuls** tend to assume a natural leadership role while **Advocates** often jump in and motivate through enthusiasm.

Extroverts have more brain activity in the parts of the brain associated with sensory input. Touch, smell, sight, taste, and sounds seem to have more impact on them. Their hand gestures tend to be more exaggerated or animated.

Introverts have an inward focus and aren't usually the life of the party. They have a strong sense of self that can make them feel highly self-conscious around other people, which in turn, can make walking into a crowded room nerve-wracking. They can be extremely witty but have a hard time being funny in front of the camera or telling jokes to more than a couple of people at a time.

Introverts process their emotions, thoughts, and observations internally. They can be social people, but reveal less about themselves to others than Extroverts do. Introverts need time to think before responding to a situation and develop their ideas by reflecting privately. Their personality traits can be passionate, but are not usually aggressive. *Mediators* tend to be more self-conscious but are more social while *Analysts* tend to be quieter and thought-centered.

Introverts can focus their attention more readily and for longer periods of time than Extroverts. Many Introverts are audio or visual learners while Extroverts are more often kinesthetic learners, meaning they tend to need to *move*. Because kinesthetic learners have to move to learn they are often mistakenly pegged as having ADHD (attention deficit hyperactivity disorder).

Some Introverts (typically the *Mediators*) aren't stereotypically shy and can strike up conversations with anyone. These Introverts enjoy talking and listening to people and going to parties and events. Generally, most Introverts would rather be at home. Some Introverts (typically the *Analysts*) can find small talk easy but tiring—and sometimes boring.

Introverts tend to get their energy from within, so being with people can be draining. After a day filled with people or activities, Introverts tend to feel exhausted and empty. To recharge their batteries, Introverts need to be alone to read, daydream, paint, or garden. Any solo activity "fills them up" again. This type of person is a great match for the horse that enjoys learning the intricate moves of dressage.

Research has shown that the Introvert has increased blood flow to the regions of the brain associated with remembering events, making plans, and problem-solving. These are *internally* focused processes. The Extrovert has increased blood flows to the areas of the brain where visual, auditory, touch, and taste sensory processing (excluding smell) occurs. These are *externally* focused processes.

This explains why the Introvert is stimulated more from within while the Extrovert needs external stimulus for motivation. When it comes to extreme sports and daredevil riding, you will usually find the participant is an Extrovert.

Recent studies have added yet a third category called "Ambiversion," though it is quite rarely seen. Ambiversion is the term used to describe people who fall directly in the middle and exhibit tendencies of both groups.

However, for our purposes here, I will only focus on people who are Introvert or Extrovert, but if you find yourself possessing equal, or nearly equal, traits from both categories, just be aware you could very well be an Ambivert.

Birth Order

The third component producing traits that make up your core Social Style is your birth order. This is defined as a person's "rank" by the sequence of birth among siblings. Some research indicates that birth order affects personality. As is true in all the other component traits, there are many variables that can change this, such as divorce, remarriage, and half-siblings, for example. However, it is interesting to look at how some of the birth-

More on Birth Order

There is a lot of available information on this concept. If you are interested in learning more, we suggest you find outside resources. Much of the birth order theory in this book was taken from online articles by Samantha Murphy or Michael Grose. While this is good information and it can certainly complement Social Styles, because our main focus is human vs. horse relationships, we have pared down this information to the basics.

order characteristics mirror traits seen in all the other components. When you start putting all traits side by side, it makes you wonder which came first: Does birth order dictate personality or is it brain function, learning method, or something else entirely?

Most of us display the characteristics that pertain to our actual position in the birth order. These traits we have from birth that make up our Social Style are called the *dominant* birth order personality traits. Any others we pick up later are *modifying* birth order traits.

The *dominant* birth order personality can be influenced by variables such as temperament, gender, and other family circumstances. For example you may find the second child acting as a first child or even an only child when there is a large gap in the number of years between two children.

We will individually discuss the *first born*, *middle child*, *last born*, and *only child* in detail below.

FIRST BORN CHILD

First born children are the leaders. Most often you will find first borns to be *Powerful*, especially when they are left-brained (fig. 3.2). They just assume the traits of a leader, especially when siblings are left in their care. When first born are right-brained they are usually *Mediators*. The first born like to manage others. They love the feeling of being in control and may be uncomfortable with surprises. They are conservative in their outlook—a strength and a weakness (fig. 3.3). Their ability to focus on a goal and their propensity to organize others means they can achieve whatever they put their minds to. (Note, see the the first born *only child* on p.44.)

A tendency toward perfectionism may indicate they can be either a low risk-taker, or, on the other hand, the rock on which a successful organization is built. Gaining approval of authority is important for this group, so don't expect them to "rock the boat" too much. Remember one of the major traits of *Powerfuls* is that they know the rules and like to follow them. First born, above all else, want to forge ahead.

Because first born children may have looked after their younger siblings, they received experience leading and mentoring others prior to adulthood. This early "training" often results in their attaining leadership positions as adults. Nearly half of all US presidents were first born children; only four were born last in their family.

First born often choose professions requiring precision, such as careers in science, medicine, law, engineering, computer science, or accounting.

MIDDLE CHILD

Middle children are the "people" people, the compromisers, and the

First Born—Traits

POWERFUL (LBE)	MEDIATOR (RBI)
• Mover and shaker	• People-pleaser
• Natural leader	• Craves approval
• Perfectionist	• Nurturer
• Is driven	• Caregiver
• Conventional	• Reliable
• Assertive	• Conscientious
• Persuasive	• Cooperative
• Always has things under control	• Team player

3.2

First Born—Strengths and Weaknesses

STRENGTHS	WEAKNESSES
• Task-oriented	• Craves approval
• Supporter of authority	• Has "grin-and-bear-it" attitude
• Energetic	• Wants things her own way
• Ambitious	• Self-critical
• Scholarly	• Inflexible
• Enterprising	• Feels she is always right

3.3

flexible operators. They are likely to be motivated by a cause and enjoy working alongside others. They will often choose tasks or even a job that give them a feeling of belonging. Friendships are important to middle children. They learn to get along with everyone and help keep the peace in a group or organization. While they often need others to drive them, the middle children are the glue holding groups together, much like *Advocates*.

Many second born are also middle children. Sometimes, they are very competitive because they have to compete with an older sibling. Others choose to focus their interest, time, and energy in areas completely different from those in which their older sibling is already established. This competition with the first born drives second children to be very inventive in their attempts to "beat" their older sibling.

Middle born children are often more competent at an earlier age than their older sibling because they learn by watching and following the older child.

Middle Child—Traits

ADVOCATE (RBE)	ANALYST (LBI)
• Outgoing	• People-pleaser
• Friendly	• Craves approval
• Loud	• Nurturer
• Doesn't follow time schedules	• Caregiver
• Flexible	• Reliable
• Competitive	• Conscientious
• Encourager	• Cooperative
	• Team player

3.4

Middle Child—Strengths and Weaknesses

STRENGTHS	WEAKNESSES
• Flexible	• Hates confrontation
• Diplomatic	• Stubborn
• Rebellious	• Cynical
• Attention-seeking	• Suspicious
• Competitive	• Rebellious
• Peacemaker	• Has low self-esteem

3.5

Because middle born children have learned to negotiate and compromise daily with their siblings and their parents, they often become very socially skilled. Some of these children are often called the "peacemakers" of the household.

Middle children can either be *Advocates* (RBE) or *Analysts* (LBI) displaying traits such as those listed in figs. 3.4 and 3.5.

LAST BORN CHILD

Last born children are the initiators, idea people, and the challengers. This group, often *Advocates*, is full of creative, live-for-the moment types who can put some fun into activities (fig. 3.6). While the message for first born might be to lighten up, it seems that this group needs to take things more seriously. Great initiators and very impatient doers, they persevere to get something started, but often are not the greatest of finishers (fig. 3.7).

Last born children tend to be the easiest to define when it comes to the correlation between birth order and personality. This is mostly due to the fact that unlike the other two, most last born children display a similar set of traits. And yet, depending on which traits are the strongest the personality could manifest as an *Advocate (RBE)* or a *Mediator (RBI).*

Last borns are generally considered the family "baby" throughout their life. Because of nurturing they have been found to be the most successful socially and to have the highest self-esteem of all the birth positions—sometimes to the point of being self-centered. However, there are some who always feel they have more growing up to do to match other family members, and these actually lack self-esteem and can become *Mediators.* When older siblings or parents take power away from these last born, they cannot make decisions or take responsibility. Because of this powerlessness, some tend to make big plans that never work out.

Last Born—Traits

ADVOCATE (RBE)	MEDIATOR (RBI)
• Outgoing	• People-pleaser
• Friendly	• Approval-craver
• Loud	• Nurturer
• Doesn't follow schedules	• Caregiver
• Flexible	• Reliable
• Competitive	• Conscientious
• Encourager	• Cooperative

3.6

Last Born—Strengths and Weaknesses

STRENGTHS	WEAKNESSES
• Risk-taker	• Immature
• Idealist	• Attention-seeking
• Has good sense of humor	• Secretive
• Hard working	• Spoiled
• Sensitive	• Self-centered
• Outgoing	• Manipulative
• Sociable	• Lacks self-confidence
• Caring	• Dreamer with no follow through

3.7

ONLY CHILD

Some only children become hypercritical, not tolerating mistakes or failure in themselves or others. They can also transform this perfectionist tendency into rescuing behavior, agonizing over the problems of others and rushing to take over and solve everyone else's troubles without allowing others to help themselves. They very easily become enablers, and above all else, only children often aim to please, thus are *Mediators.*

Only children are also the quiet achievers, the finishers, and expect nothing less than the very best from themselves. This group will raise the bar for everyone around them as "nothing but the best will do" is the expected contribution from others as well. One of their greatest strengths is to work independently for long periods of time. They make excellent project finishers and strategic thinkers, thus are *Powerfuls.* They can be secretive at times and don't deal well with conflict. Recognition is important to this group (figs. 3.8 and 3.9).

Only children may also demonstrate characteristics of first

Only Child—Traits

POWERFUL (LBE)	MEDIATOR (RBI)
• Mover and shaker • Natural leader • Perfectionist • Driven • Conventional • Assertive • Persuasive • Always has things under control	• People-pleaser • Approval-craver • Nurturer • Caregiver • Reliable • Conscientious • Cooperative

3.8

Only Child—Strengths and Weaknesses

STRENGTHS	WEAKNESSES
• Organized • Follows the rules • Responsible • Has a clarity of purpose • Perfectionist • Stable	• Self-centered, seeks attention • Fearful of trying new things • Self-critical • Worrier • Inflexible • Feels she is always right

3.9

born and/or last born. First born, after all, are only children until the next sibling is born.

They may rely on service from others rather than exert their own efforts. They sometimes please others if it suits them, but still may also be uncooperative. They may also have been over-protected by their parents, giving them a false sense of security.

TEST YOURSELF

After reading this chapter and reviewing fig. 3.10, which birth order personality do you most closely resemble? Does it match your birth order position? In reality, you probably nodded your head for some characteristics in each position. With which personality did you most vigorously nod in agreement while reading the description? Whichever one you most "resembled" is the one that will give you an indication of your *dominant* birth order Social Style.

Learning Method

Have you ever wondered why you just can't seem to remember names? Why you can't learn to dance easily? Or maybe why you tap your feet to a song but others don't? It could be the way you learn, which is the fourth component that influences your core Social Style. While it does not have a one-to-one correlation to horses, understanding this can impact other aspects of your life. This is especially true if you (or your children) are students. But regardless, it can just be fun to know your learning style.

There are actually three basic methods of learning—*kinesthetic, auditory,* and *visual*—though were you to research learning methods further, you would find many offshoots of these. However, for the purpose of this book, we will stick to the basic ones. People usually have one—or two—dominant methods of learning, but can use all three styles. People may prefer one method of learning for one task, and a combination of others for a different task. If you don't possess all three styles, there are ways to compensate.

Of course, like the four core Social Styles, a *balance* of all three of these methods makes learning easier. This is because information comes at you in all forms and if you were to limit your learning methods, you'd limit your learning.

Birth Order: Summary of General Traits

First Born	Middle Child	Last Born	Only Child
Energetic	Mediator	Risk-taker	Organized
Ambitious	Flexible	Idealist	High achiever
Enterprising	Diplomatic	Has good sense of humor	Responsible
Scholarly	Rebellious	Hard-working	Self-centered
Craves approval	Attention-seeking	Immature	Perfectionist
Nurturer	Competitive	Attention-seeking	Attention-seeking
Reliable	Strives for peace	Secretive	Natural leader
Conscientious	Analyst	Sensitive	Scholarly
Cooperative	Impatient	Adventurous	Has difficulty sharing
Team player	Encourager	Impulsive	Has trouble accepting others ideas
Natural leader	Outgoing	Manipulative	Dependable
Perfectionist	Friendly	Smothering	Inflexible
Assertive	Loud	Interacts well with others	Impatient
Wants things her way	Easy-going	Resistant to structure	Conscientious

3.10

A person on the *active* end—someone who likes to move when learning—is the *kinesthetic learner*. A person on the *passive* end is the *auditory learner*. The *visual learner* is somewhere in between.

You're probably thinking, "Great, so how do I know what I am?" Remember, as with birth order, it is rare for someone to have traits from only one learning style; most people have traits from all the different styles in varying degrees. And, as you know, sometimes these traits can be at odds with each other. Understanding which learning method you prefer and how to compensate for your weaker methods will help you set yourself up for success (just like understanding your horse's learning styles will help you set him up for success).

For example, if you know your weakest learning style is auditory, you wouldn't select a CD in order to learn a new topic.

Not only is it valuable for you to know how you learn, it is equally important to know how others learn. If you are going to teach a person how to ride a horse, is it better if you tell her, show her, or let her do it hands-on? Or, when you are trying to sell a horse long distance, will the potential buyer understand more about the horse if you tell her about him over the phone or send her something in writing?

Most people give you clues in the way they speak. For example, a person will say, "I *see* what you mean" when she is a visual learner, or "I *hear* you," when an auditory learner. However, if you can't tell, by all means, ask her. She can probably tell you if she learns better by *doing, hearing,* or *seeing*.

KINESTHETIC LEARNERS

Given a choice, kinesthetic learners will often sit near the door in a classroom. Children with this learning style are often labeled "troublemakers" or thought to have ADHD. They are the kids who tap their pencil, move around in their chair, and constantly move their leg, tapping their feet. They drive the teacher crazy, disrupt the class, and because of their behavior are punished, constantly told to sit still, or may be prescribed medication. But the fact is, once this type of person "sits still," he or she quickly becomes bored and stops learning.

This type of learner benefits greatly from being allowed to move around. The trick is to find something that doesn't disrupt other types of learners. I have found that providing kinesthetic learners things like silly putty or doodle pads can help the learning process.

If you are a kinesthetic learner, it's very likely you use your body and sense of touch to learn about the world around you. You probably like sports, exercise, and other physical activities like cleaning stalls in your barn. You like to think out issues, ideas, and problems *while* you exercise. Some of your best problem-solving is done when you go for a ride, run, or walk.

Sitting is not a good "thinking" position: When forced to sit to think, you will tap your foot, fill in all the circles on the paper in front of you, or find some other way to move.

When learning a new skill or topic, you prefer to "jump in" and play with the "physical parts" as soon as possible. For example, you prefer to pull an engine apart and put it back together, rather than reading or looking at diagrams about how it works. Just the thought of sitting in a lecture "listening" to someone else talk is boring. In those circumstances, you fidget or can't sit still for long. You want to get up and move around.

To determine if you are a kinesthetic learner, ask yourself whether you agree or disagree with the following statements:

- When learning how something works, I like to take it apart.

- I have a hard time paying attention when I am required to sit for a long time.

- When I see something interesting, I want to touch it to learn more about it.

- I tap my feet when I listen to music.

What if you are also an *Advocate*? You are more sensitive to the physical world around you. For example, you notice and appreciate textures in clothes or tack. You enjoy "getting your hands dirty," or actually building the stalls rather than just planning or overseeing their construction. You typically use larger hand gestures and other body language to communicate.

If you couple this learning method with a *Powerful* personality who can't focus on details for very long, you end up with someone who can't even focus on a movie. She can watch the same movie several times and still enjoy it. This occurs because sitting still for two hours causes a *Powerful* to lose focus and only "see" about half the movie. Because of this lack of focus, she sees something new every time. *Powerfuls*—with this kinesthetic learning style—especially have trouble remembering book or film titles, and author, performer, and artist names.

It is not so common for true *Mediators* and *Analysts* to be kinesthetic learners because they don't have such a need to move. However, remember most people are a combination, so if you score high in one of those categories and are a kinesthetic learner, you are likely to have the need to move but with less exaggerated movements.

VISUAL LEARNERS

Visual learners are those who learn through their eyes. These learners need to see the teacher's body language and facial expression to fully understand the content of a lesson. They may think in pictures and learn best from visual displays including: diagrams, illustrated text books, videos, and all manner of photographic materials. During a lecture or classroom discussion, the visual learner often prefers to take detailed notes. This is not the least active learning method and works well for those people who are more balanced with introverted and extroverted traits.

Visual learners prefer using images, pictures, colors, and maps to organize information and to communicate with others. They can easily visualize objects, plans, and outcomes. This learning style often shows up in right-brained people. I have a friend who can "see" how a room will look before it is painted and decorated. This trait seems to fit **Advocates** particularly well.

Visual learners usually have a good sense of direction, easily finding their way around using maps. This trait goes well with the **Analyst** Social Style. When trail riding, the visual learner instinctively knows which way to turn. This comes in really handy when you are riding a horse that always has to lead. We have all been with people who can ride down a trail, make one turn and then not be able to find their way back. Now you know it isn't that they are not intelligent, it's their learning style!

Given the choice, visual learners would rather use email to "talk" to others and avoid phone conversations. Have you seen the cartoon of the dog owner talking to his dog on the phone? There is a "bubble" over the dog's head indicating that the dog is hearing, "Blah, blah, blah, Spot, Blah, blah, blah."

This could be compared to how true visual (and kinesthetic) learners hear a phone conversation. Of course, even though they don't actually hear "Blah, blah, blah," they just can't focus on what is being said. Nor can their mind link whatever is being said to any reasonable "format" and they can't follow a train of thought. It is probably unwise to give complicated information over the phone to this type of learner.

One very interesting point is you can often recognize this learning method by the words people choose to use. Visual learners say, "Look" "See," "Draw it out," "Can't picture it." "I see what you are saying," is another example.

TEST

To determine whether you are a visual learner, ask yourself whether you agree or disagree with the following statements:

- When I sit in a classroom, church service, or theater, I prefer to sit in the front so I can see better.

- When I build something, I need to see pictures or diagrams.

- When I am told how to do something, I remember it better when I take notes.

- When I go somewhere new, I need a map to find it.

AUDITORY LEARNERS

Auditory learners learn best through verbal lectures, discussions, talking things through, and listening to what others have to say. Auditory learners interpret the underlying meanings of speech by listening to the tone of voice, pitch, speed, and other nuances. This type of learner will usually sit at the back of the room, as "seeing" too much is disruptive. Even the facial expressions and body language of the instructor can distract the auditory learner. This is the least active learning style and is often found in Introverts.

Written information may have little meaning as they prefer oral forms of communication. These people often benefit from reading text aloud or using a tape recorder. They prefer talking on the phone to reading letters or emails—

when reading a letter or email, they feel they miss its *inflection* because there is no "voice" to it. They often understand as much by "how" something is said as by "what" is said. This can be a big problem when so much information today is communicated via email, texting, and other platforms on the internet. Because of the brief nature of these new methods, misunderstandings can occur with consequent hurt feelings that weren't intended. Nevertheless, the auditory learner is the person to whom most school systems cater!

Auditory learners love reading and writing but will often read aloud or listen to books on tape. They find it enjoyable playing around with the meaning or sound of words, such as tongue twisters, rhymes, and limericks. They are very good at crossword puzzles. Auditory learners usually have a great vocabulary, regularly making an effort to find the meaning of new words and use them.

TEST

To determine whether you are an auditory learner, ask yourself whether you agree or disagree with the following statements:

- When communicating with someone at a distance, I prefer the telephone to email or texting.

- When looking at instructions, I read them out loud.

- When given an assignment, I prefer to work with others.

- When I listen to music, I tend to hum along.

Much like visual learners, you can tell an auditory learner through several key words. Auditory learners will use words and phrases like "talk," "hear," "spell it out,", and "I hear what you're saying." An advantage of being an auditory learner is you are very good at remembering names.

Summary of Learning Methods

Kinesthetic Learner	Visual Learner	Auditory Learner
Must be moving around and use sense of touch to learn	Learns by sight	Learns by listening
Is more aware of details in the world around her	Learns best by reading	Listens for tone of voice and nuance
Uses more body language	Is good at visualizing what something will look like	Likes to read out loud
Uses bigger hand gestures	Has good sense of direction	Can sit and listen for long periods of time
Likes to take things apart	Needs to see instructor's facial expressions	Prefers to talk on phone vs. email
Gets bored and shuts down when having to sit too long	Likes pictures, diagrams, color charts	Very good at remembering names
Enjoys sports and high energy activities	Takes detailed notes	Enjoys learning with others

3.11

LEARNING: MALE VS. FEMALE

There is scientific proof (based on medical technology) that the male brain and the female brain function differently in many ways. Some schools have started implementing single gender classrooms as a result of these findings. Preliminary results are showing grades improve and behavior problems decrease at these schools.

You will see an overlap here between the previously discussed learning methods. In fact, we view the different male and female brain function as the basis for learning, with kinesthetic, visual, and auditory as modifiers.

Here are some differences between the sexes. While not every male and female reacts this way, it is a good place to start for a quick, general assessment.

First, men see things differently than women. The male eye is drawn to cooler colors like silver, blue, black, grey, and brown. A much higher percentage of males are color blind. The female eye, on the other hand, is drawn to both textures and colors. Women are drawn to warmer colors like reds, yellows, and oranges. They are also drawn to visuals having more detail, like faces. Boys will tend to draw cars in dark colors, while women will draw families and flowers in happy colors. Why is this important? If you are giving a business presentation to all men—use appropriate colors. If you are teaching in gender specific classrooms, gear your teaching to accommodate their core learning methods.

The male's eye is attuned to motion and direction. When you want to teach something you need to move around the room constantly: a moving object to capture his attention.

Females work well in circles facing each other. The teacher doesn't need to move to have their full attention. It is also known that females are more able to engage in multi-tasking behavior, use both sides of the brain when processing information, and often hear better than males.

Males may take more time in processing emotive information, thus making it more difficult for them to quickly adjust after engaging in stressful or emotionally charged situations. For example, a male who had an argument with his spouse before leaving for a board meeting will not be able to focus and learn while he is still upset. When he understands this concept, however, he can often find an activity like a quick workout to lower his stress level before going to work.

A woman can have the same argument with her spouse and still be able to focus and learn at her normal level. (Interestingly enough, a horse is like the male: when the horse is upset or scared, he will not be in a learning mode.)

The male brain needs activity to learn, often doing things like tapping pencils or flipping the book cover back and forth. This is why we associate kinesthetic learning more often with males than with females. Males learn better when there is space to spread out and there is noise in the classroom. Studies show males score higher when allowed to do a good physical workout before testing. It's not the same case with females at all.

Males typically give directions using the North/South/left/right types of directions, while females more often give directions using landmarks.

An interesting point to note is that everyone's brain is made up of four lobes. The front two function as the logic-control center for thinking and learning. The back two function as the emotion-control center for flight- and fight-type responses. Females appear to be able to engage all four lobes at the same time. In other words, they can be scared or angry but *still* use the logic part of their brain for logical thinking and learning. Males do not seem to engage all four lobes simultaneously. When they become angry, they can no longer use the logical part of the brain until their anger or fear has subsided.

CHAPTER 4

The Four Human Social Styles—In More Depth

N THE LAST CHAPTER we covered a lot of information about the four components that help to define human personality:

1 Left and Right Brain

2 Introvert and Extrovert

3 Birth Order

4 Learning Method

All of these contribute the traits that make up the four core personality Social Styles: *Analyst; Powerful; Mediator; Advocate*. We introduced these Styles briefly in chapter 1. Now that you understand the components that contribute to the personality traits, here is a composite look at each Social Style.

Analysts (LBI)

Analysts are people who take their time to collect all the details and will have all the facts. Their traits include:

- Liking to work alone.
- Preferring a quiet setting.
- Doing their own research rather than asking questions.
- Presenting their work in spreadsheet format.
- Being logical.
- Having difficulty making the final decision.

Note: Both types of Introverts (*Analysts* and *Mediators*) have trouble making decisions but for a totally different reason: *Analysts* because they might find more information later, and *Mediators* because they don't want to hurt anyone's feelings.

Analysts are sometimes considered absent-minded because they get so caught up in the details they occasionally forget everything else.

It is most common to find the *Analyst* with *Powerful* as her primary modifier because both Socials Styles are left-brained. *Analysts* who are very good at their job can find they get promoted when the *Powerful* side of their personality enables them to head a team successfully.

Sometimes it can be hard to determine the difference between the two Social Styles. The key is in the amount of detail that comes naturally to the *Analyst* and the fact that a *Powerful* may do better with people and focus more on goals.

There is actually a fairly fine line between them even though the *Analyst* is an Introvert (likes to "ask") and the *Powerful* an Extrovert (likes to "tell"). This is because while *Powerfuls* are indeed Extroverts, they are not as extroverted as *Advocates*: they do fine with big crowds but also enjoy quiet times.

Likewise, an *Analyst*, normally not keen on crowds, can revel in an audience when presenting detailed information.

ANALYST COMBINATION PERSONALITIES

Core style plus modifiers:

1 *Analyst/Analyst*: Pensive, logical, detailed, methodical. They are totally thought-based and introverted.

2 *Analyst/Powerful*: Pensive, logical, detailed, methodical, impatient, quick, abrupt, goal-oriented. They are thought-based and both introverted and extroverted.

3 *Analyst/Mediator*: Pensive, logical, detailed, methodical, accommodating, friendly, compliant, subservient. They are both thought- and emotion-based as well as introverted.

4 *Analyst/Advocate*: Pensive, logical, detailed, methodical, overly enthusiastic, dramatic, and see the "big picture." This person is thought- and emotion-based as well as both introverted and extroverted.

When an *Analyst* is "forced" into her "Z" pattern (see p. 15), she will first go from *Analyst* to *Powerful* (both Left Brain but Introvert to Extrovert), then to *Mediator* (Left to Right Brain and Extrovert back to Introvert), and finally to *Advocate* (crossing all boundaries). This means that a Left Brain Introvert *(LBI)* becomes a Right Brain Extrovert *(RBE)* under extreme stress.

When your *Advocate* score (from the questionnaire in chapter 2) is close to your *Analyst* score it could mean:

1 You are an *Analyst* under stress.

2 You are a fairly balanced *Analyst*.

3 You are an *Analyst* that has had to become an *Advocate* because of your job function or another outside influence.

When an *Analyst* has a low score in *Powerful*, slightly higher score in *Mediator,* and almost equal in *Advocate* you could be in the process of stressing. Only you will know for sure if you are stressing, well-rounded, or being forced to take on traits for outside reasons—your job, for instance.

If you are still uncertain, we suggest you go back to the lists of traits and select those that best describe you in a totally relaxed situation. That should clarify exactly which Social Style you are—an *Analyst* actually stressing or just well-rounded.

Remember your core Social Style is made up of traits from the four components, of which Left or Right Brain, and Introvert or Extrovert are the first two. So while an *Analyst* is a LBI, not every trait is seen in all left-brained individuals, nor does every trait of an Introvert fit every *Analyst*. The chart in fig. 4.1 shows these two components' traits that are unique to the *Analyst*.

Analyst Component Traits

LEFT BRAIN	INTROVERT
• Logical	• Quiet
• Rational	• Draws energy from within
• Objective: to make decisions on facts and data	• Reserved
• Detailed	• Forms deep, close friendships
• Quiet	• Prefers to be alone or with one or two close friends
• Fact-oriented	• Problem-solver
• Makes and checks off lists	• Remembers important dates
• Does tasks in order	• Is good at coordinating activities
• Follows directions easily	• Low-keyed
• Good with math and science	• Organized
• Wants to know the rules	• Private

4.1

Powerfuls (LBE)

Powerfuls are people who get others moving to meet the deadline! Here are a few of their traits. They:

- Don't want too much detail.
- Make decisions quickly.
- Lead people to reach a goal.
- Are goal-oriented.
- Are good presenters and communicate well.
- Are logical.

Powerfuls, extroverts who normally "tell" others will "ask" questions when something is of specific interest or, more commonly, because they want to maintain control like, "Did you get that report done?" They "tell" more often than they "ask." They are usually high-energy types (but not to the extreme of *Advocates*) and are good at thinking ahead.

It is most common to find *Powerful/Analysts* because they are both left-brained and, therefore, logical. *Powerfuls* get bored easily so it is difficult for them to go deep into details unless they are very interested in the topic when their *Analyst* side kicks in with a detailed analysis.

Another example of a combined style are *Powerful/Advocates*, who are not so involved with details: they only seek enough information to "control" a project. These combination-style people have the tendency to cheer their team on toward achieving a goal. They combine logic (Left Brain/*Powerful*) and emotion (Right Brain/*Advocate*), and are the ones who are more people-oriented leaders. Since both styles are Extroverts they are good in high-profile situations.

When a *Powerful* becomes involved with detail, it is to control the project. When an *Advocate* becomes involved with detail, it is most often because she

Powerful Component Traits

LEFT BRAIN	EXTROVERT
• Logical	• Outgoing
• Rational	• Draws energy from the people around
• Objective	
• Makes lists and checks items off	• Assertive
	• Thinks best on feet
• Follows directions easily	• Self-confident
	• Friendly
• Good with math and science	• Tuned-in to environment
• Makes master schedules	• Works best in groups
• Works from "parts" to "whole"	• Enthusiastic
• Gives directions in compass headings and miles	• Enjoys sensory events
	• Easy to get to know
• Is a good communicator	• Is open with feelings
• Persuasive	
• Uses the word "think"	

4.2

has an extreme passion for what she does, such as clothing design or other creative activities. (Note: A *Powerful Advocate* is different from an *Advocate Powerful*.)

POWERFUL COMBINATION PERSONALITIES

Core style plus modifiers:

1 *Powerful / Powerful*: Impatient, quick, abrupt, goal-oriented because they are totally thought-based and extroverted.

2 *Powerful / Analyst*: Impatient, quick, abrupt, goal-oriented, pensive, logical, detailed, methodical because they are totally thought-based, and extroverted or introverted ("tell" as well as "ask").

3 *Powerful / Advocate*: Impatient, quick, abrupt, goal-oriented, overly enthusiastic, dramatic. They see the big picture because they are thought- and emotion-based and extroverted.

4 *Powerful / Mediator*: Impatient, quick, abrupt, goal-oriented, accommodating, friendly, compliant, and subservient because they are thought- and emotion-based and extroverted or introverted.

When a *Powerful* is forced into her "Z" pattern she will go from *Powerful* to *Analyst* (both Left Brain but Extrovert to Introvert), then to *Advocate* (Left Brain to Right Brain and Introvert back to Extrovert) and finally to *Mediator* (crossing all boundaries). This means that an LBI becomes a RBI under extreme stress.

When your *Mediator* score is close to your *Powerful* score it could mean:

1 You are a *Powerful* under stress.

2 You are a fairly balanced *Powerful*.

3 You are a *Powerful* that has had to become a *Mediator* because of your job function or another outside influence.

When a *Powerful* has a low score in *Analyst*, slightly higher in *Advocate* and almost equal in *Mediator,* you could be in the process of stressing. Only you will know for sure if you are stressing, well-rounded, or being forced to take on traits for outside reasons.

Remember your core Social Style is made up of traits from the four components, of which Left or Right Brain, and Introvert or Extrovert are the first two. So while a *Powerful* is an LBE, not every trait is seen in all left-brained individuals, nor does every trait of an extrovert fit every *Powerful.* The chart in fig. 4.2 shows these two components' traits that are unique to the *Powerful*.

Mediators (RBI)

Mediators are people who want to please. They:

- Assume they should do the work.
- Need to feel appreciated.
- Like to work in small groups of close friends.
- Want everyone to be happy.
- Are good with details.
- Remember special occasions.
- Have trouble making decisions.

They will take on everything (sometimes more than they can handle) to please others and to avoid getting "yelled at." They are probably the nicest people you will ever meet and tend to be unable to say "no." They often have trouble making a decision for fear someone will be unhappy with it. When you are talking to a *Mediator* on the phone, make small talk before you get to the actual point—selling a horse, for example.

It is most common to find *Mediator/Advocates* because they are both right-brained. A *Mediator* might get caught up in the moment and become an *Advocate*, going from Introvert to Extrovert ("telling" rather than "asking"). While they are Introverts by nature, many *Mediators* enjoy being in big crowds. The *Mediator* trait of "attention to detail" makes them great people to organize social events. The *Advocate* side of the personality can also help them attend and maintain control of events.

MEDIATOR COMBINATION PERSONALITIES

Core style plus modifiers:

1 *Mediator/Mediator*: Accommodating, friendly, compliant, subservient. They are totally emotion-based and introverted.

2 *Mediator/Advocate*: Accommodating, friendly, compliant, subservient, overly enthusiastic, dramatic, big-picture. They are emotion-based and introverted or extroverted depending on the situation.

3 *Mediator/Analyst*: Accommodating, friendly, compliant, subservient, pensive, logical, detailed, methodical. They are emotion- and thought-based and introverted.

4 *Mediator/Powerful*: Accommodating, friendly, compliant, subservient, impatient, quick, abrupt, goal-oriented. They are emotion- and thought-based and introverted or extroverted. It's more common to find a *Powerful/Mediator* than a *Mediator/Powerful* as it is easier to cross from being an Extrovert ("telling") to Introvert ("asking") than the other way around.

Mediator Component Traits

RIGHT BRAIN	INTROVERT
• Feeling	• Quiet
• Random	• Draws energy from within
• Intuitive	• Reserved
• Creative	• Forms deep, close friendships
• Subjective: makes decisions on personal views and opinions	• Prefers to be alone or with one or two close friends
• Looks at whole then works to parts	• Problem-solver
• May have trouble finding the right words to express herself	• Remembers important dates
	• Is good at coordinating activities
• Flexible	• Low-keyed
• Says "feels right"	• Organized
• Uses landmarks when giving directions	• Private
• Learning	

4.3

If a *Mediator* is forced into her "Z" pattern, she will first go to *Advocate* (both Right Brain but Introvert to Extrovert), then to *Analyst* (Right Brain to Left Brain) and finally to *Powerful* (crossing all boundaries where an RBI becomes an LBE).

When your *Mediator* score is close to your *Powerful* score it could mean:

1 You are a *Mediator* under stress.

2 You are a fairly balanced *Mediator*.

3 You are a *Mediator* who has had to become a *Powerful* because of job function or another outside influence.

If you are a *Mediator* and have a low score in *Advocate*, slightly higher in *Analyst* and almost equal in *Powerful,* you could be in the process of stressing. Only you will know for sure if you are actually stressing or are just well-rounded.

Remember your core Social Style is made up of traits from the four components, of which Left or Right Brain, and Introvert or Extrovert are the first two. So while a *Mediator* is an RBI, not every trait is seen in all right-brained individuals, nor does every trait of an Introvert fit every *Mediator*. The chart in fig. 4.3 shows these two components' traits that are unique to the *Mediator*.

Advocates (RBE)

Advocates are people who encourage others to work together toward a sense of team and accomplishment. They:

- Are cheerleaders.
- Make decisions quickly.
- Are "artsy"
- See the big picture.
- Have high energy.
- Have a dry sense of humor and enjoy trivia.
- Enjoy being the center of attention.
- Do *not* enjoy detail.

Punctuality is something for everyone else. It is more fun to arrive fashionably late so others will notice them. They are very creative and often are involved in fashion, art, decorating, and similar careers.

It is most common to find an *Advocate/Mediator* personality blend as both are right-brained. The *Advocate* might find a topic she is really excited about, like art or fashion; however, she might need the *Mediator* modifier to pick up the details. This person would also be good at directing a play. She remembers special events and is the one doing the "fun" stuff like getting a clown for a birthday party (or even arriving as the clown herself).

ADVOCATE COMBINATION PERSONALITIES

Core style plus modifiers:

1 *Advocate/Advocate*: Overly enthusiastic, dramatic, sees big picture. They are totally emotion-based and extroverted.

2 *Advocate/Mediator*: Overly enthusiastic, dramatic, sees big picture, accommodating, friendly, compliant, subservient. They are emotion-based and both extroverted and introverted (will "tell" and "ask").

3 *Advocate/Powerful*: Overly enthusiastic, dramatic, sees big picture, impatient, quick, abrupt, goal-oriented. They are both emotion- and thought-based but extroverted.

Advocate Component Traits

RIGHT BRAIN	EXTROVERT
• Philosophical	• Outgoing
• Feeling	• Draws energy from the people around her
• Random	
• Intuitive	
• Creative	• Assertive
• Subjective: makes decisions on personal views and opinions	• Has several surface level friendships
	• Enjoys large groups of acquaintances
• Looks at "whole" then works to "parts"	• Motivator
	• Tuned-in to environment
• Flexible	• Works best in groups
• Daydreams	
• Likes sports	• Enthusiastic
• Needs to feel, see, touch, smell	• Good at giving presentations
• Says "it feels right"	• Easy to get to know
• Uses landmarks when giving directions	• Open with feelings
	• Enjoys sensory events
• Flits from task to task	• Naturally responsive with people

4 *Advocate/Analyst*: Overly enthusiastic, dramatic, sees big picture, accommodating, friendly, compliant, subservient. They are both emotion- and thought-based and extroverted and introverted.

If an *Advocate* is forced into the "Z" pattern she will first go to *Mediator* (both Left Brain but Extrovert to Introvert), then to *Powerful* (Right Brain to Left Brain) and finally to *Analyst*—crossing all boundaries, making an RBI into an LBI.

When your *Analyst* score is close to your *Advocate* score it could mean:

1 You are an *Advocate* under stress.

2 You are a fairly balanced *Advocate*.

4.4

3 You are an *Advocate* who has had to become an *Analyst* because of job function or other outside influence.

If you are an *Advocate* and have a low score in *Mediator*, slightly higher in *Powerful,* and almost equal in *Analyst* you could be in the process of stressing. Only you will know for sure if you are stressing or are just well-rounded.

Remember your core Social Style is made up of traits from the four components, of which Left or Right Brain, and Introvert or Extrovert are the first two. So while an *Advocate* is an *RBE*, not every trait is seen in all right-brained individuals, nor does every trait of an Extrovert fit every *Advocate*. The chart in fig. 4.4 shows these two components' traits that are unique to the *Advocate*.

The Whole Human

Pulling all the components together, let's take a look at the example of Molly. She scored 15 as an Extrovert, 3 as an Introvert, 12 for Left Brain, and 10 for Right Brain. She is primarily a *Powerful (LBE)* with a total score of 27. She also has *Advocate (RBE)* modifiers (tendencies) with a score of 25.

As we start to build the list of Molly's personality traits we are going to list all the attributes she *could* have. In real life, you would then need to look at Molly and eliminate those traits that don't fit.

So let's analyze Molly. Since she is almost all Extrovert she won't have many introverted traits because she only scored 3 on that side. She has a higher left-brained score, but only by a small margin. Consequently, she will likely show a good balance from both (see chart of traits on p. 34).

From the entire list of traits, the following describe Molly. From her *Powerful* side, she is logical, rational, assertive, self-confident, friendly and outgoing. She does tasks in order, makes master schedules, draws energy from people around her, tunes in to her environment, and works best in groups. From her *Advocate* side, she is creative, flexible, likes sports, and is enthusiastic.

Now let's throw in her birth order. Molly is a last born child. This could explain the combination of *Powerful* and *Advocate* characteristics. Last born children typically are risk-takers, idealistic, attention-seekers, sensitive, and hard workers. The risk-taker's and hard worker's attributes point to the *Powerful* personality, while the idealistic, attention-seeking, and sensitive traits point to the *Advocate* personality.

How to Apply This Book to Real Life

Know You, Know Your Horse is not just about finding the right horse and training him as best suits him; it also offers valuable lessons you can apply in other parts of your life. Wondering what else this book is good for? Here are just a few areas you'll find can be improved with what you learn on these pages:

- Sales (and remember, *everybody* sells—even the child trying to "sell" his parents on the idea of letting him go someplace with his friends).

- Parent-to-child relationships.

- Spouse-to-spouse relationships—understanding your partner's personality goes a long way to preserving your relationship. It helps explain the little things, like: Why does my husband watch the same movie 15 times? And why doesn't he enjoy shopping for birthday cards?

- Instructor-to-student relationships—when the trainer understands human learning styles and how best to communicate with a particular student, the lesson will go more smoothly and the student will learn more easily. This applies to all teaching scenarios, whether in a riding arena or a school classroom.

- Parent-to-teacher relationships.

- Employee-to-employee relationships.

- Employer-to-prospective employee (and vice versa)—understanding personality is a good skill to have both for the interview process and in terms of hiring the right person for the job. (For example, you might not want to hire a *Mediator* for a help desk where he or she is going to be dealing with a lot of angry customers—the *Mediator* likely will not be able to handle the pressure.)

- Team-building—when you are working in a group or creating groups for specific purposes, knowing each person's personality helps you combine strengths and offset weaknesses to your best advantage.

- Nursing, hospice work, counseling services.

Molly is a *kinesthetic learner*. This too points to an ***Advocate*** personality. ***Advocates*** will typically use more body language and larger hand gestures when talking. This need for body movement carries over into her learning style. Kinesthetic learners are the ones who need to tap a pencil, doodle, play with a toy, or maybe shake their leg to learn. Like most Extroverts, she also gets bored quickly. Molly could have easily been misdiagnosed as having the disorder ADHD as a child.

Molly's ***Powerful*** side makes her a good candidate for a management position but her ***Advocate*** side might keep her from sticking to a timetable. While Molly could be successful in many careers, with the balance she has she would probably be a good teacher. She could use her ***Powerful*** nature to keep order in the classroom and her ***Advocate*** side to relate to and motivate her students.

In Conclusion

Not every person has every trait on the list of attributes for each component. Over time, all people learn what works for them—and what doesn't. They keep the traits that make them successful and drop the others.

When you meet new people, go ahead and make a quick judgment based on the information presented in this book. It will help you with "surface" relationships such as those with sales people, acquaintances, and other members of a team at work. However, for a lasting relationship, take the time to really get to know the person to make a full analysis.

PART TWO

The Horse Personality

CHAPTER 5

Getting to Know
the Horse

A S EXISTS FOR HUMANS, there are four core personality styles for horses. These are called *Thinker (LBI)*, *Worker (LBE)*, *Actor (RBI)*, and *Talker (RBE)* and their Social Styles complement human Styles—in this order: *Analyst (LBI)*, *Powerful (LBE)*, *Mediator (RBI)*, **and** *Advocate (RBE)*. (See more about this in the Social Style Grid—fig. 5.1.)

The traits that make up the four different horse Social Styles are those associated with these four components: *Introvert/Extrovert; Left Brain/Right Brain; Herd Order;* and *Learning Method.* A horse's conformational characteristics can affect personality, too. All are discussed in more detail in chapters coming up.

Why is it a good idea to determine a horse's personality? There are four basic situations where knowing and understanding the personality of the horse is helpful.

1 You want a horse that will be your friend: one that is as excited to see you as you are to be with him. If you choose a horse with traits contrary to yours, it can be difficult to form a bond so you want a horse that matches your personality. When that doesn't happen, you will probably spend less time doing the things you want to do with him.

2 You want to participate and be successful in a specific discipline: you not only will need to be aware of the horse's conformation, but also his personality. For example, just because you buy a Thoroughbred with good conformation, doesn't mean he will want to go fast—his personality plays a big role as well. Some call it "heart." So you need to get a horse with the personality to be successful and be aware he may not match you, and you may be required to modify your personality to get along with him.

The Social Style Grid

THINKER (LBI)	WORKER (LBE)
Left Brain (Fight instinct)	Left Brain (Fight instinct)
Introvert ("Wants" to keep his feet *still*)	Extrovert ("Wants" to keep his feet *moving*)
ACTOR (RBI)	TALKER (RBE)
Right Brain (Flight instinct)	Right Brain (Flight instinct)
Introvert ("Needs" to keep his feet *still*)	Extrovert ("Needs" to keep his feet *moving*)

5.1

3 You want to rescue an abused horse. This is where your ability to understand personality really comes into play. A horse that has been starved may change quite a bit once he is "fattened up." And one that has been severely abused may be very reactive to certain stimuli—his core personality may not be what you first see when he is rescued. You may be required to modify your personality several times as you work him back to his "original" personality.

4 You want to train horses. Understanding different horse personalities and having the ability to align with them will make you more successful. Not all horses understand things the same way. Some horses need to *move* to learn while others need time to *stop and think*. Knowing the difference is key. You will need to modify your personality from horse to horse.

Just like people, horses have core personalities and modifiers. Unlike people, horses rarely cross over the Introvert and Extrovert boundary, and the

The Four Horse Social Styles

THINKER (LBI)	WORKER (LBE)	ACTOR (RBI)	TALKER (RBE)
Inventive (will open gates)	Will work all day	Reserved (may have no facial expression)	Can be vocal (yells for his buddy)
Loves standing	Friendly (likes to play)	Devoted (acts like he wants to be "in your pocket")	Impulsive (overly quick in actions)
Food-oriented	"Nippy" (likes to put his mouth on you)	Can be very intense	Hyperalert (overly active when fearful)
May be stubborn	Willful	Distrusting	High-headed
May charge or kick when fearful	Pushy (wants to go)	May be unpredictable	May panic: bolt or rear
May buck when upset or in play	May bite or strike at something that upsets him	May freeze (stop and lock up) then explode—rear, bolt, spin—in fear	Feet need to move when frightened
Is careful with novice or handicapped rider	Is confident with novice rider	Is precise when he trusts rider	Will go anywhere when he trusts rider

5.2

differences between Left and Right Brain are less obvious. Nevertheless, there are still four very distinct types of horse Social Styles (fig. 5.2).

As far as the rider is concerned, perhaps the most important component making up the horse's personality is whether or not he is introverted or extroverted (for more about introverted vs. extroverted horses, see p. 89).

The right- and left-brained traits, often just a matter of the way the horse reacts, relate to degrees of survival instinct. The strength of his flight or fight instinct determines how extreme his right- or left-brained trait will manifest itself, which can also be influenced by his age and training.

The left-brained horse is typically more suitable for the novice or rider with less experience, while the right-brained horse generally needs an experienced rider or a confident one with less experience (for in-depth discussion of left- and right-brained horses, see p. 90).

When answering the questions in the Horse Personality Questionnaire below, it is critical to be honest about your horse. Do not view any of his traits as negative. Every trait makes that horse perfect for a specific job. For example, if he has a defiant personality, it makes him a perfect horse for the mounted police: he can stand his ground when an officer rides him into the middle of an angry crowd.

If you already own or know a horse well, this questionnaire will help you determine his personality. However, when you are looking at a horse to buy, you may need to have the current owner help you fill out the answers, or failing that, a good trainer who understands horse personality.

Horse Personality Questionnaire

There are 24 pairs of statements in the Horse Personality Questionnaire. As in the Human Social Style Questionnaire (p. 22) you need to pick one item from each pair that best describes the most typical behavior of your horse. You may have never seen your horse do one of the actions but try to use your gut instinct that tells you "he would do one of these," then pick the behavior that fits.

Circle the chosen item's number where it appears under the four core personality styles listed under the questions, or photocopy the page; jot your answers down on a separate piece of paper; or download the questionnaire from the *Know You, Know Your Horse* page on the Trafalgar Square Books website (www.horseandriderbooks.com).

Make your choice as spontaneously as possible.

TEST

1. My horse gets frustrated when I want him to stand still.
2. When coming upon something new, he will stop and smell it.

   ─────────

3. My horse is "mouthy."
4. He likes being in a group.

   ─────────

5. My horse likes to see the tail of another horse in front of him.
6. He has a lot of endurance.

   ─────────

7. My horse likes to race.
8. He will work for food.

   ─────────

9. My horse runs and runs when he's turned out.
10. He enjoys trying to find ways to escape.

    ─────────

11. My horse learns through repetition.
12. He influences the behavior of other horses in a group.

    ─────────

13. My horse can be defensive.
14. He is receptive.

15. My horse likes to "go."
16. He likes going slowly.

    ─────────

17. My horse likes new and different things.
18. He is unpredictable.

    ─────────

19. My horse is distrustful of many people.
20. He is smart.

    ─────────

21. My horse values treats over any distraction.
22. He has a tendency to run.

    ─────────

23. My horse understands best when an exercise is repeated several times in succession.
24. He gets bored easily.

    ─────────

25. My horse can be pushy when he's nervous.
26. He will paw when he wants something.

    ─────────

27. My horse will think before he does anything new.
28. On the longe line he anticipates coming back in from the circle.

29. My horse moves really quickly when he is frightened.
30. He is unconcerned about new things.

31. My horse thinks anything around the barn is something to play with.
32. He spooks easily.

33. My horse can spin on a dime.
34. He goes more slowly the more you push him.

35. My horse does not like being held to a walk.
36. He does better with a gentle hand.

37. My horse doesn't like to back up.
38. He doesn't come when called.

39. My horse enjoys new tasks.
40. When startled by another horse or human he will kick.

41. My horse can be over-reactive.
42. He is stubborn.

43. My horse rears when scared.
44. He easily forgives humans for their mistakes.

45. My horse bucks or paws when upset.
46. He is timid.

47. My horse likes to be told where to "put his feet."
48. He doesn't like to move sideways.

Questionnaire Scoring Chart

Extrovert (E): 1, 3, 6, 7, 9, 15, 22, 26, 28, 35, 37, 48

Introvert (I): 2, 4, 5, 8, 10, 16, 21, 25, 27, 36, 38, 47

Left Brain (L): 12, 14, 17, 20, 24, 30, 31, 34, 39, 42, 44, 45

Right Brain (R): 11, 13, 18, 19, 23, 29, 32, 33, 40, 41, 43, 46

Results

Left Brain Introvert *(LBI)* = **Thinker**

Left Brain Extrovert *(LBE)* = **Worker**

Right Brain Introvert *(RBI)* = **Actor**

Right Brain Extrovert *(RBE)* = **Talker**

5.3

SCORING

Scoring the horse's personality is slightly different from the way you score your own (see p. 25):

1 Take the numbers of your 24 answers to the questionnaire and locate them in the chart containing numbers that relate to Extroverts, Introverts, Left and Right Brain traits (fig. 5.3).

2 In numerical order, write the numbers down and place an **E, I, L, R** next to each one, depending on which line of numbers you find it. For example, taking a random sample of six numbers, you would write: 1E; 4I; 6E; 17L; 34L; 43R (and so on).

3 Next, calculate the total number of each of the letters to discover if your horse is a Left Brain Introvert *(LBI)*; Left Brain Extrovert *(LBE)*; Right Brain Introvert *(RBI)*; Right Brain Extrovert *(RBE)*. For example, if you have *LBI 11; LBE 13; RBI 5; RBE 19*, then the horse's highest score is *RBE 19*, which designates his core personality as a ***Talker.*** His next highest score, his primary modifier, is *LBE 13*, a ***Worker.*** (These designations are contained in the chart on p. 80.)

On the pages that follow, we'll present a brief description of the four core horse Social Styles: ***Thinker, Worker, Actor,*** and ***Talker.*** Following these are several "real" horse personality descriptions, and in the next few chapters, the foundation traits from the four components—Extrovert/Introvert; Left/Right Brain; Herd Order; and Learning Method—that make up the personalities are discussed in a great deal more detail.

Horses, like people, often cross into other styles or may not display every trait within their core personality. Here are a few descriptions to help you better understand your horse. First, we'll look at the two horse personalities with a higher "*fight* instinct": the **Thinker** and the **Worker**.

"Fight Instinct"

Thinker (LBI): As the name implies, this horse likes to "think" about things. He is confident but likes time to dwell on decisions. When on the trail and he comes to a split in the road, he may need to stop and think about which way to go. If you force him, he will hold his ground and not move. The **Thinker** can become bored with arena work but does find stimulation in obstacles. When asked to do the boring work, he can appear to be asleep or just very dull. This horse loves to stand and be groomed. He may seem to drag behind you when you're leading him. Many successful **Thinkers** are seen as police mounts, therapy horses, or roping horses. The **Thinker** *wants* to keep his feet still. (For more on the **Thinker** and how to train him, see p. 193).

Worker (LBE): This horse will work all day. He is confident and makes good decisions on his own. The **Worker** can be willful. When riding down a trail and coming to a split, he may decide—on his own—which way to go. He can get bored very easily doing work in the arena. When doing groundwork, he wants to "lead you" instead of walking with you. The **Worker** thrives in any riding discipline that allows him to make choices. Many successful **Workers** are seen cutting cows or show jumping. The **Worker** *wants* to keep his feet moving. (For more on the **Worker** and how to train him, see p. 203).

Now let's look at the two horse personalities with a higher "*flight* instinct": the **Actor** and the **Talker**.

"Flight Instinct"

Actor (RBI): This horse is not always what he appears to be. He may look quiet when, in reality, he is a worrier. He needs a confident yet subtle rider to work with him because when scared, he can react differently every time. The *Actor* rarely gets bored: he likes and finds comfort in routine—going along slowly. When doing groundwork, be sure to talk to him before walking up behind as he might kick out without thinking. *Actors* can be successful at dressage and Western pleasure—among other riding disciplines. They *need* to keep their feet still. (For more on the *Actor* and how to train him, see p. 213.)

Talker (RBE): This horse is outgoing and often vocal about finding his buddy. He needs a good, confident rider to keep him from running away. He can be very quick in his reactions. The *Talker* rarely gets bored, and he likes lots of speed. However, in order to concentrate on groundwork—and stop him invading your "space"—he needs repetition. *Talkers* can be successful at long-distance competition, reining, and gymkhana / contesting events, to name just a few. The *Talker needs* to keep his feet moving. (For more on the *Talker* and how to train him see p. 221.)

Now let's look at some real examples of each horse personality style.

Rosie

Rosie's questionnaire scores are *Extrovert 3; Introvert 21; Right Brain 4; Left Brain 20.*

What do these numbers say about Rosie?

Rosie is a definitely a *Thinker (LBI).*

Rosie's scores mean she gets bored easily, needs lots of rest time, and is food oriented. However, when content, she will be confident and curious.

When she was a filly her introverted side would cause her to be the one in the pasture that tired quickly when running with the other foals. If the other "babies" tried pushing her into playing, she would start bucking and send them off. She was happy to just go back to eating grass. As she matured, her introverted side caused her to enjoy adventure but not long training sessions.

Her high-scoring left-brained results mean that Rosie spends quite a bit of time being playful and clever: figuring out how to open various gates with her mouth and pull off other horses' fly masks. They also contributed to her finding training when young easier. When asked to face a new object all you had to do was let her smell it, think about it a minute, and then proceed.

Her low-scoring points (4) on the right-brained side means she will spook momentarily, but will quickly think it through and then show more curiosity than fear.

Rosie became a cow horse. She was very clever at working her way into a herd of cows, cutting out one, and pushing it to the pen. When her turn was over she would stand at the trailer and take a nap.

Dante

Dante's questionnaire scores are *Extrovert 20; Introvert 4; Right Brain 10; Left Brain 14.*

What do these numbers say about Dante?

Dante is a **Worker** (LBE).

Dante's scores indicate he wants to be in control of his pasture buddies and his trainer. Therefore, like other horses of this type, he usually needs a more confident, experienced rider. He doesn't like to stand still and often wants to take off before his rider is ready.

The nearly even split in his right- and left-brained scores indicates he is confident but can lose focus easily, wanting to go too fast at times.

Having high points on both the Left and Right Brain made early life for

Dante interesting. The 14 left-brained points gave Dante a very high play drive and some self-confidence, but this coupled with an almost equal 10 points on the right side, caused him to swing from being bossy to being worried and nervous. He could be confident in familiar surroundings, but when things were new it took him a while to settle down.

As a confident foal, this Extrovert would run into the barn and loop back around the pasture before settling for a short time by his dam, during which time he nipped at her when she just wanted to rest. Once weaned, he became the dominant colt; he would bite and even strike at the other colts to make them move when he wanted.

With such a low Introvert score, he didn't display many traits from this category (p. 89).

Dante was eventually paired up with a confident, experienced owner who was a successful eventer. He could barely tolerate the hour of grooming required to get him ready for a show (a sign of a horse with few Introvert points), but once he was on the course, it was his passion. With the extensive varied training schedule that eventing requires, he enjoyed the sport and all it had to offer. When he got a bit too hasty or worried during a competition his owner could take control and calm him down with ease.

Casper

Casper's questionnaire scores are *Extrovert 11; Introvert 13; Right Brain 14; and Left Brain 10.*

What do these numbers say about Casper?

Casper is an *Actor (RBI)*.

Casper has 13 points in the Introvert and 14 points in the Right Brain category so he is only barely an *Actor*. However, with this balanced personality

Casper is definitely an exceptional horse. His right-brained side may indicate fear but his Left Brain keeps it short-lived. The extroverted traits give him the endurance to show all day as long as there aren't speed events, and his introverted side keeps him calm for mounting and grooming.

Casper is an older horse. Many years of good training, handling, and experience have brought his scores into nice balance. Being only slightly more of an Introvert, he is quieter, less concerned, and willing to stand. With almost an equal amount of Extrovert he enjoys a good run, but it isn't something he wants to do all day.

Casper wasn't always this balanced. When his training started he was much more *RBI*. While he was eager to get started, he was also very nervous when his trainer asked for something new. His first trailer ride left him sweating and nervous, but with that ride and many to come, his owner gave him a good rub and talked quietly until he settled. When riding him, his owner knew to breathe deeply to help Casper relax and breathe too. His owner would slow down the approach and give him time to calm his emotions and be brave again. Eventually this kind of treatment brought Casper closer to the *LBI* horse that is interested in his surroundings, confident, and well balanced.

Casper was very successful in Western pleasure. He loved all the grooming on show day. It was like having a wonderful massage under his owner's hands. In the beginning, the hardest part of showing was horses coming up to pass him. He would pin his ears and if they were too close, he wanted to kick them! He is long past that behavior now.

Years of experience and an owner who continually matched her personality to his has allowed Casper to be confident and stay focused on his rider. He is not concerned about the other horses. For his owner he is a "dream," seeming to sense without any aids what speed to go and exactly where to put his feet. Together, they also enjoyed hunter and trail classes.

Star

Star's questionnaire scores are *Extrovert 20; Introvert 4; Right Brain 18; Left Brain 6.*

What do these numbers say about Star?

Star is an "extreme" **Talker** *(RBE)*. "Extreme" means she has a distinct core personality with high scores in both Extrovert and Right Brain. The closer these two scores are to a total of 24, the more extreme her personality is.

Her scores mean she will have forward motion with speed if allowed. She is always alert.

When Star was a filly she often ran into the back of her dam. When weaning time came, she was very vocal about her fears of being away from her mother. Once settled in with other younger horses, they would all run the fence lines together, and she was often seen rearing up in play. Her high extrovert points gave her energy to run fast but not always focusing on where she was going. "Whoa" was the most difficult thing for Star to understand and accept.

High right-brained points made Star a very over-reactive mare. She was always alert to what was happening around her, and her instinct always told her to "run"!

Star was lucky enough to be sent to a trainer who understood how she processed information. It is only because of this good training that she has (2) points on the Left Brain or confident side. Star needed to be trained in the same manner, day after day, repetition after repetition.

Star became a gymkhana/contesting horse. Her favorite event was pole bending. The poles were always 21 feet apart and there were always six poles. Star knew this pattern and could run as fast as she wanted without being held back.

CHAPTER 6

Four Components That Define
Horse Personality

Introvert vs. Extrovert

Understanding the concepts of the first component that makes up the horse's personality—Extrovert or Introvert—is a critical key to aligning horse and human.

Let's take a look at some horses riding through a campground as an example. Someone in your group has just encountered the dreaded campground trash bin on an introverted horse.

If he is a *Thinker* (*LBI*), he might come across the trash bin and do nothing at all, presumably thinking to himself, "Oh, there's a trash bin, so what?" If he is a *Thinker* but a bit more curious, he might meander over to take a sniff just in case it holds some treats. (If you are riding this horse and he stops to look, just let him stand for a few minutes, then ask him to proceed.)

But when your horse is an *Actor* (*RBI*), he is no doubt still standing a quarter mile away thinking, "There is a tiger in that bin, and it will jump out and get me." You don't know exactly how this horse might react: he may blow and snort, then skitter past the bin, or blow and snort and run the other way. (It's best to dismount this horse and use an approach-and-retreat method of getting to the trash can.)

Now let's look at that same encounter with an Extrovert.

The *Worker* (LBE) horse would probably walk right up to the bin and plan to rearrange whatever might be in there, thinking, "I'm sure there's something of interest here, if not, I'll just go on past it." (If this horse seems concerned just look forward, ask him to go on ahead, and give him verbal reward for doing so.)

When your horse is a *Talker* (RBE), he might see the bin, and with urging from you, head that way. However, be careful because he is probably thinking, "I know if I can run past it very fast, the tiger will not get me. I just have to be fast enough." (When you have this type of horse, be ready to ride quickly past the bin many times until he calmly walks by. Whatever you do, don't ask him to stop and look until he is ready.)

Right Brain vs. Left Brain

The old expression, "Lead, follow, or get out of the way," could have been written just as easily about the horse as the human. It fits perfectly for the way the equine mind works.

The left-brained horses—*Workers* and *Thinkers*—think before they react. A *Worker* wants to be in the lead. He is happiest when he can set the speed of travel. The *Thinker*, on the other hand, isn't as concerned about speed but is very curious and wants to check out everything along the way. The *Thinker* will want to stop and "put his nose" on the object.

The right-brained horses—*Actors* and *Talkers* are more reactive. The *Actor* may stop suddenly and snort, or he may spin and run; while the *Talker* will pick up speed and try to run past the perceived threat.

These traits are what make a horse in tune with the right person. So how do you determine whether a horse is right-brained or left-brained?

In humans, we consider the right side of the brain emotional, and the left part the logical side. It is similar with horses—except they can't deduce or reason. However, they do have an emotional component: it's called "instinct."

The instinct component drives every other aspect of the horse except the desire to move his feet or to keep his feet still. The right-brained horse may be more nervous or worried. He is the horse that jigs and sweats easily. He is usually very athletic. The higher alert type horse is even farther to the right-brained side. He will tend to spook more easily, depend more on the herd for safety, and need a secure rider. Some will even display physical traits such as their veins showing (popping up) even when they are not working; their eyes show a lot of white; or they may look as if they are squinting. A right-brained horse will almost always go into "flight" mode more easily.

At the other end of the spectrum is the left-brained horse. This horse may be more playful and curious and is not as quick in his reactions. The extreme example may *seem* more logical, but it's really more a matter of his being less likely to go into "flight" mode. These types of horses "think" about what is happening before they decide whether they need to fight or flee, and some may get a reputation for having more of the "fight" mode in them. Regarding physical traits, they normally have a large round eye and a bit wider forehead. They are not generally as attuned to where their feet are. Stallions in the wild that survive are usually much more left-brained, ready to fight when need be to protect the herd.

Let's use an encounter with a Mylar balloon as an example.

When you tie one to a barrel, the left-brained horse will see the balloon and watch it move. He may stop and take a look, go up and even try to touch it with his nose, or he may just trot on by, looking interested but not worried about it at all. He will be calm and rational about the experience.

The right-brained horse will view the balloon in a much different way. He may stop to look but will also snort, maybe jump backward, even though he may still be a distance from the balloon. He may appear nervous to the point of shaking. This horse may try to spin and bolt with no real thought of direction or his surroundings.

Both types can be wonderful horses. We don't want you to walk away from a horse just because he shows fear. Understanding the personality of your horse and how you or the trainer's personality can make any horse your "dream horse" is very important.

But, when you match a worried horse with a worried trainer or rider, there is a very good chance things will go bad. And if you match a worried horse with a trainer or rider who is too heavy handed, it could also go bad. However, when you match a worried horse with a confident, fair trainer or rider, you can have an excellent result.

Herd Order

While horses may not have a birth order, they certainly have a herd order. When discussing herd dynamics, we are talking about a "family."

WILD HERD

A "wild" herd usually consists of the main stallion, younger stallions usually under the age of six, mares, and foals. "Domestic" herds have been changed by humans to fit their needs and can consist of any combination. To truly understand the domestic herd, you must first understand the wild one.

When a wild herd is on the move, you may not see the stallion leading his "harem." His job is to tend to the mares and keep his herd safe. He must be strong, smart, defend and fight for his mares and foals, as well as keep the young stallions safe.

The *Worker (LBE)* is a good candidate for herd leader as he has a high level of endurance and the will to fight. However, the heightened awareness that comes with the Right Brain component is also necessary to be the herd's leader. This is an example of "modifiers" as you read about in the human personality analysis, evolving naturally in horses due to environment and stresses.

Next in line is the lead mare. She is usually one of the oldest and smartest horses in the herd. It is her job to direct the herd to watering holes or safety as needed: whenever the stallion is away, she must stay alert for any threats and quickly decide if the herd should run. The mare may be seen off to the side rather in the middle of the herd so she has a clear view of the surrounding area. She fights to remain dominate and is often seen getting the best grass or making other herd members move. This mare needs a good balance of personality styles and components. She needs to be left-brained in order to think through situations, but not so far in the left-brained direction that she cannot see a threat quickly enough to react. The best horse for this role is a *Talker (RBE)* with *Worker (LBE)* modifiers.

Each wild herd consists of a variety of personalities. It is this combination that makes the herd successful. However, it is the stallion and the lead mare's personalities that determine how long and how well the herd survives.

DOMESTIC HERD

This is not the case in domestic herds. The personality of the owner can determine the personalities of the mares and stallion. For example, one farm that we visited during the writing of this book bred Quarter Horses for racing. The owner was an *Analyst*. When I asked her how she selected her breeding stock for purchase, she said she first looks at cost, bloodlines, and conformation, but once she narrows it down to the final few, she picks the horses that "like" her. This told us she was selecting Introverts. We then went to her barn and did a personality assessment on her herd. Both of her stallions were Introverts. Next, we went to the field to do assessments on the mares with foals. While we found both right- and left-brained horses, all were Introverts. This herd would have had difficulty existing in the wild.

When looking at a domestic herd you may see all geldings, all mares, or a mix. This is an "unnatural" herd. However, through an understanding of the dynamics in a wild herd, you can avoid injury to your horses. For example, a gelding turned out with a mare may still have his stallion instincts and become aggressive toward any additional horses. But put the same gelding out with other geldings and he may be quite relaxed: as a rule, in such groups, there are rarely big battles for "top spot." Usually there is just a lot of body language and an occasional nip or kick.

Mares are not as easy. People often think you can put any horses together and they will get along. This may happen, but if it doesn't, you can end up with an injured horse. So how do you successfully put mares together? Let's assume the lead mare already there is a *Talker (RBE)*. A *Talker* is a high energy horse that will read and can be very intimidating in a herd. Here is what often happens when you introduce her to a:

- *Thinker (LBI)*: Being slower and food-oriented this mare may not fight unless it is over food. However, if they were to fight, the *Thinker* would not think twice about charging right into the *Talker*.

- *Worker (LBE):* Also a highly energetic horse, she might react by biting or striking at the lead mare.

- *Actor (RBI)*: This mare would most likely try to stand away, but if cornered she might spin around and kick.

- *Talker (RBE)*: This could be a major battle of wills because both have the same traits, in particular, endurance and speed.

This is where personality modifiers along with age, experience, and desire come in to play. Any one of these horses could take the lead position with enough experience and desire, but the Extroverts tend to have more desire to push for the lead position. So you can see how in horses, as in humans, the components that make up Social Styles can make a big difference in how they find their place.

Turning out your new horse into an existing herd can be a challenge. The last thing you want is to have to call the vet to do a bandage job, or worse, something more serious. My suggestion, when possible, is to put a new horse for a few days into a separate area: small paddock, round pen, or even a stall. I would use an electric fence between them for at least a day.

Allow the herd to get the scent of the new horse. Be sure that when they are where they can touch each other that they don't get legs caught in round pen panels or wood fences. After a day you can take down the electric fence and allow them to smell each other. Watch for the interaction. You may see ears pinned, or hear a bit of "screaming," but it shouldn't take long before they all go back to grazing or at least ignoring the newcomer. When the situation looks as if it is becoming "violent," give them more time separated but close. Note: For your own safety, stand away when introducing loose horses.

In the wild, horses in the herd have their battles, and they either find a place to fit in or they must leave. In domesticated herds, horses don't have the option to "leave." Therefore, you must be aware of your horses' personality so horses don't get hurt. Continuing to turn a horse out with a lead horse that won't accept him could result in broken bones or deep wounds.

Learning Method

EXTROVERTED HORSES

When you are training, the *extroverted* horse, whether **Worker** or **Talker,** will either "want" or "need" to *move* his feet.

The **Worker** *(LBE)* "wants" to move his feet. If you try to hold him back he will lose focus, become bored and agitated. But if you ride him with confidence and do not make a big deal out of a fearful object, the **Worker,** given the freedom to choose, will usually handle most situations. If he does speed up when going past a threat, you can circle him around and ask him to walk past it again. Forcing this horse to "stop" will have him pushing through on his own and probably pulling the reins out of your hands. You'll have more success if you allow him to be part of the decision process.

The **Talker** *(RBE)* "needs" to move his feet. When training him (or just riding) and you try to hold him back he will react with fear. This can include bolting or rearing. The **Talker** better handles a fearful situation when you look ahead and not at the object that is bothering him. Put him in a steady walk and go past with some energy. Have some contact but do not pull him up with the reins. You may have to repeat this a few times until he is willing to slow or stop to look. Controlling the direction of his feet, not the speed, is better for the **Talker.**

INTROVERTED HORSES

The *introverted* horse, "wants" (**Thinker**) or "needs" (**Actor**) to *stop* his feet.

The **Thinker** *(LBI)* "wants" to stand and think before reacting to anything. When you try to force this horse to move faster than he wants in a situation, he may react by locking up and refusing to move, or even bucking. He will better handle a fearful situation when you allow him to stop, look, and sense the object before then asking him to move on up to and past it.

The *Actor (RBI)* "needs" to stop his feet, but at a farther distance from the object. He needs quiet comfort from his rider and rubbing to calm him down, keeping him from going into a panic. He will better handle the situation when you stop his feet and don't ask him to get too close, too quickly. When he braces up, the best thing is to dismount if you can. Speak to him gently and give him a rub, ask him to stand for a minute and then walk him past the source of fear, then remount. If you can't dismount, plan to turn around and go farther away to a point he "can" stop his feet. Calm him down, and then ask him to walk forward again. Approach and retreat is imperative to this horse. He needs to deal with frightening situations in small sessions.

It is important to remember that when the horse's brain is in flight or fight mode he is impossible to teach. When your horse is terrified, angry, or upset, you are not going to be able to force him to focus.

The more left-brained the horse is, the more passive. When you need to train or ride your horse through an unknown situation, understanding the difference in personality is very important. The more right-brained, the more he will be "emotionally" active.

Let's revisit the situation of a Mylar balloon discussed earlier. The different approach you take when working with left-brained or right-brained horses will determine your success. Left-brained horses are more curious or "thought-based" where right-brained horses are more fearful or "emotion-based."

LEFT BRAIN

When the horse is left-brained, the balloon can already be in the arena or you can have it brought in by someone. This horse can handle it either way. Let the horse see the "whole picture" and allow him to decide in what way to handle it. The left-brained horse is more curious.

A *Thinker* will more than likely want to stop and look, and then approach and smell.

The *Worker* will either walk right up to it to play or want to just look as he passes.

RIGHT BRAIN

When the horse is right-brained, you will want the balloon to either be at the opposite end of the arena, or have someone come in from the opposite end holding the balloon. The more right-brained horse can react to fear in different ways. Working with him through confident, quiet language and calmness will make accepting things easier.

The *Actor* will need to stop and look from a farther point. Let him stand and think about it, then ask him to take a few steps toward the balloon. If he tightens up he should be allowed to retreat, calm down, and then be asked again until he is confident.

The *Talker* will need to be moving, just control the direction of his feet. Whether it is to circle forward toward the balloon or circle back away from it depends on his needs. Continue this until you feel him calm down and accept the approach to the balloon.

The Whole Horse

Now let's pull all these traits together to see the whole horse. We will call him Jack. Jack is a *Worker (LBE)* who through good training has become well balanced. His core personality was to be pushy, playful, and not stand for mounting. As a colt, he was friendly, sometimes too friendly. He didn't understand or respect your "space." He would walk right over you if you were not forceful enough. He was mouthy and you were never sure if he would rub on you or nip. If you slapped his nose, he would become even more willful.

When watching Jack play with his pasture buddies, you most likely would see Jack running up to another horse, striking out with his foot, and then trying to bite him.

A good trainer was able to understand Jack's personality and determine which discipline was most likely to succeed with Jack. Jack's *Worker* personality lends itself to eventing, cross-country, cutting, and liberty games. If you're looking for a safe trail horse able to go all day, this is the horse for you. The trainer just had to wait and see what type of person would come along for Jack to complete his training by discipline.

Because Jack gets bored very quickly, training had to be creative. Correct training included lots of constructive play, including games that had Jack speed up, slow down, make turns, and go again. Frequent new lesson plans are a must for Jack.

Being a *Worker* Jack would act up now and then on the things he wasn't wild about doing. Working on the longe line, he would go along fine, then abruptly stop and strike out or kick out. When this happened, the best thing to do was be confident, laugh at him, then push him to go faster. If you punish this horse for bad behavior, he will get mad and prove to you he can be even worse. It's deflating to him if you laugh and push to go faster. He gives up and goes about his work.

Jack was very lucky his trainer understood him. Jack did not care for backing up, moving laterally, or standing still for anything or anyone! If Jack had been forced to do these tasks, he may have done them but would have been hateful about it.

The trainer who worked with Jack did most of his training on the trail or in an outdoor arena. At most, he would spend 30 minutes a day in the inside arena noting Jack's tolerance for this training. Some days he went the full hour inside, other days only 10 minutes. Instead of going around and around the arena, the trainer set up barrels and cones and would ride him around the wall a couple times, then go to the barrel or around a cone, then ask for up and down transitions along with a couple steps back. This would help Jack to tolerate the backing and turning on the forehand without seeming to be forced. He even saw this as a game and enjoyed it.

Once outside, the trainer would take Jack on a nice long trot down the trail, stop to get off to look at something, then ask him to stand for mounting. Once remounted he would rub Jack's neck; ask him to flex his nose back to his boot, reward him; then maybe ask him to step back a couple steps, and then let him walk off.

Over time with the correct training, Jack learned to balance what he wanted to do with what he needed to do to become a good riding companion. The Extrovert side of Jack would always be there; he would always love going forward more than anything, but Jack also learned to become a balanced Extrovert. He found it wasn't so bad to stand for his rider to get on after all. He learned he would get to move his feet soon enough and all would be well.

IN CONCLUSION

When selecting a horse, training makes all the difference in the world. A horse can be any core personality but when the trainer works with him according to his personality—not by using a "cookie-cutter" method of training—a horse can become "balanced" and happy.

CHAPTER 7

Physical Characteristics:
Effects on Personality

Conformation Analysis

In addition to the information presented in the last chapter, there are other clues to a horse's personality type. These are his facial features and his swirls; there is often a correlation between appearance and character. The horse is a prey or flight animal by nature. The placement of the eyes or the ears can affect his potential for survival. For example, in the wild, horses that cannot see or hear very well are in more danger than those with acute vision or hearing. A horse with vision or hearing difficulties tends to be spookier and lacking confidence, making him right-brained.

One of the main things to understand in regard to facial analysis of the domestic horse is that each breed has a conformational standard (check breed association websites for individual breed characteristics). Therefore, just saying that a horse's eye is small may well be inaccurate because that may be the standard size for his breed.

Each breed has basic differences. In some cases, you need to physically compare horses. If you stand an Appaloosa next to an Arabian, you will notice the Appaloosa has smaller eyes, and a larger jaw and ears. These alone don't distinguish a personality trait because they are within the breed standard for Appaloosas. However, if you were to compare one Appaloosa to another and noticed one with smaller ears and eyes, these differences could definitely be an indication of personality.

Breed standard is not only conformation but also temperament. Each type of horse is typically bred with a specific job (or jobs) in mind. These jobs dictate the conformation and temperament strived for by breeders. Unfortunately for many horses, breeders don't always understand what effect the conformational changes they are breeding for will do to the personality and temperament of the horse.

It doesn't matter which type of horse you want, as long as you understand that breed's standards. Only by knowing how the horse *should* look, can you determine if there is a conformational difference that might affect his personality. When you decide which horse interests you, take or find pictures of "champions" or a photo of the standard. Get to know the conformation of the breed so you can compare it to the horse you are considering for your own.

FACIAL FEATURES

To understand how conformation affects the personality, let's discuss the horse's head. The following is a list of characteristics that may vary within the confines of individual breed standards.

- Large tufts in the ears: possibly a sign of inflexibility and a strong will (left-brained).

- Ears longer and narrower than breed standard: may be inconsistent (right-brained).

- Floppy ears (if not a pain issue): a dependable horse (left-brained).

- Wide-set ears tell you he is a kind horse.

- Ear tips almost touching each other indicates a very clever horse. You may be thinking, "Great, I want a smart horse," but are you experienced enough to deal with a horse that is one step ahead of you?

- Forehead extremely wide between the eyes: may be very intelligent; willful (left-brained).

- Forehead extremely narrow for the breed: may be slower to learn but very dependable once he understands his job (right-brained).

- Wide-set, large, soft eyes placed well on the outside of the head, but visible from the front or the side are preferable. Large eyes give the horse a wider viewing area. Eyes placed correctly give the horse the ability to go from *monocular* vision (vision in which each eye is used separately) to *binocular* vision (vision in which both eyes are used together), allowing him to see a predator.

- Deeply dished head: very sensitive and timid (normally very right-brained).

- Bulges or bumps on the head—as in Roman nose; or an Arab with a large bulge above a deep dished head: a difficult personality (cross between left-brained and right-brained extremes).

- Eyes higher on the head than normal: slow learner (Introvert).

- Softness in the eye is an indicator he is not in pain and has a calm temperament (left-brained).

- Small jowl: lacks confidence, harder to train, will take more time (Introvert).

- Straighter profile and larger jaw indicates the horse is easygoing (left-brained).

- A large dip in the nose: this may inhibit lung capacity or breathing, which in turn, can change a personality and make a "flightier" horse. In the wild, a horse that can't keep up or runs out of breath is the first one to fall to a predator (right-brained).

- Extremely long and narrow nose: usually slow to learn (right-brained and introverted tendencies).

- Large nostrils indicate better lung capacity, especially important for endurance sports. Large nostrils also allow the horse to gain more "scent" information, often resulting in less spookiness (left-brained).

- Large nose but flaring nostrils: thinks a lot but is nervous (right-brained).

- A mustache on the nose, which you won't see too often: horse will be a very kind and easy ride for even the least experienced riders (left-brained).

- Flapping lower lip: may be a slow learner (right-brained).

- Mobile upper lip: enjoys human contact (left-brained).

SWIRLS

It is believed that hair swirls are developed at the same time as the nervous system is formed in a foal in utero. Most horses have one swirl that sits between, or slightly above, the eyes. Horses with different swirls can mean a modified personality.

- Below the eyes: indicates imagination and character; very curious and will spend much time trying to figure out how to open a stall door or a gate latch (left-brained).

- Long single swirl between the eyes divided evenly up and down: enjoys being with humans; good indicator for a child's horse (left-brained).

- Two swirls sitting side by side: oversensitive (right-brained).

Measuring Techniques

The distance between the eye and the ear, and the eye and the cheek bone, should be almost the same. This is easy to measure and is another method many trainers use to select an intelligent, calm temperament.

The Arabs have a technique with their Arabian horses to tell if the horse is smart, athletic, with a good temperament. They take some string, run it from the tip of the nose up around the ears and back to the nose. The measurement should be the same as when you run the string from the hoof to the withers.

So as you can see, even if you have perfect conformation, little things like tufts of hair in the ears, a mustache or an odd swirl, just to name a few, may indicate the personality of your horse and should be considered in his training.

The characteristics listed in fig. 7.1 are only examples; they do not mean that every horse with one of these traits will have a particular personality. Treat the information as yet another piece of the personality puzzle.

Physical Characteristics and Traits

CHARACTERISTICS	PERSONALITY TRAIT
Forehead extremely wide between the eyes: may be very intelligent, but also willful.	Left Brain
Forehead between the eyes extremely narrow for the breed: will be slow to learn. Once this horse understands his job, he is very dependable.	Right Brain
Eyes higher on the head than normal: can be a slow learner.	Introvert
Ears longer and narrower than breed standard: inconsistent.	Right Brain
Tips of ears are very close set: very intelligent and very quick to react.	Right Brain
Ears flop to the side: if not a pain issue, a dependable horse.	Left Brain
Head deeply dished: very sensitive and timid.	Right Brain
Overly long and narrow nose: can be slow to learn.	Introvert
Medium to small jowl: lacks self-confidence and is harder to teach.	Introvert
Flapping lower lip: slow learner.	Introvert
Mobile upper lip: enjoys human contact.	Left Brain
Large nose with flaring nostrils: a nervous horse.	Right Brain

7.1

The key to finding a horse is first to pick one that matches your personality and your desired discipline. His physical appearance is just another quick indicator when you look at a field full of horses from which to choose.

Before you go horse shopping, decide what type of horse you want and take the time to study and understand the breed standards. As mentioned, all these specific qualities are available on individual breed websites. The more you understand every aspect of a breed, the better you can compare your selection to the standards and the better the horse matches, the better chance you have of finding your perfect mount.

Note

For further detailed information about features and how they affect the horse's personality, we recommend the book *Getting in TTouch: Understand and Influence Your Horse's Personality* by Linda Tellington-Jones. Some of the information we presented here comes from her book.

PART THREE

Matching Human to Horse and Horse to Human

CHAPTER 8

Putting It All Together

Selecting a Match

You should now have a pretty good idea of how to identify both your own and your horse's personality. It's time to make a decision. Do you want to select a horse as a riding partner or do you want him for a specific discipline? If the former, you should look for a horse that matches your personality. If you don't and you fall in love with your "opposite," you will need to learn how to work inside his personality. And, if you want to excel in a specific riding discipline, you may well need to be willing to adjust your Social Style to fit the type of horse that can do the job.

Either way, if you decide to get a horse and the "match up" doesn't work, you need to be willing to do one of the following:

- Change your core personality when dealing with him.

- Work with a trainer that understands this horse and can help you in matching him until he aligns with you, though it's possible this could be a long time—even years—and in some cases may not happen at all.

- Keep the horse as a pet if he doesn't "work out."

- Sell the horse and find one that is a match for you.

Remember, every time you handle or ride your horse, you are dealing with his core personality: if your horse likes to go slowly and you like to go fast—it's just too bad—and should you keep "pushing" him, there is a very real potential that problems will result. Over time, some horses are able to change their personality through training, but you can't always count on that, and in fact, it might even appear that he has changed, but when things go really bad, the horse's core personality traits will always come back to the forefront.

Matching Personalities

Analyst = Thinker (LBI)	**Powerful = Worker** (LBE)
Mediator = Actor (RBI)	**Advocate = Talker** (RBE)

8.1

In some cases, a horse's behavior will get worse because you are trying to force him into something he's not suited to handle. When you are ready to make a long-term commitment to a horse, you need to decide if you want to find the perfect match or if you can deal with the differences. Should you decide to live with the differences, you will need to change to be compatible with your horse or be willing to live with the consequences of a mismatched trait or traits.

When you are looking for that perfect match, first select the horse that mirrors your personality based on the Introvert or Extrovert component. Then evaluate your personal level of confidence. If you don't know how confident you are, it is useful to work with a trainer, riding instructor or someone who is knowledgeable enough to help you decide. This knowledge will help you determine the need for a right- or left-brained horse or the amount of professional training you may need before you are ready for this horse.

To start, we'll examine the characteristics of the human Extrovert and Introvert and then look at the characteristics of the horse Extrovert and Introvert, and finally, how they mesh.

HUMAN EXTROVERT

There are two types of extroverted humans: *Advocates* and *Powerfuls.*

Extroverts are usually satisfied as long as there is speed—a good fast walk will do. An Extrovert is not one who cares if a horse will "stop and put his nose" on an object. As long as he gets past what he needs to and gets the job done, the Extrovert is happy.

Extroverts will always look at a horse because he is "pretty." They want their horse to be naturally beautiful at all times. They do not like to spend much time on the details of grooming at all. They usually prefer their horse to be full of energy, and go all day. An Extrovert tends not to enjoy groundwork as much as the Introvert.

Advocates (RBE) are energetic and outgoing, and they especially enjoy "thrill" riding: anything that includes speed or competition. They are often seen at endurance races along with contesting or gymkhana events, among others.

Powerfuls (LBE) are energetic and goal-oriented. They are likely to want to take a long ride with a specific trip in mind and will stay focused on the trail, its landmarks and the final destination. *Powerfuls* like doing everything at a fast pace. This doesn't mean they will do it at a run, but they want a horse that has plenty of forward movement. They don't usually stop and stand for long periods of time, nor do they have a need to mosey down the trail. A

Powerful is likely found on cross-country rides, and at eventing and jumping competitions.

Extroverted riders are known to have bigger body language; they may not be as gentle and quiet with their hands. They are forceful and use more pressure with their hands and legs than introverted riders. They "talk" with their hands; tend to hang on the reins more; and exert more pressure with their legs. Their horse needs to be able to handle these exaggerated hand and body movements.

There are two types of extroverted horses: the *Worker* and the *Talker*. When the extroverted person is a less confident rider, a novice, or has health issues, she might look for the *Worker*. Both human and horse types still have the urge to achieve a goal with some speed but want to do it safely. The *Worker* horse is confident, and he may be "opinionated," but he will never let you get lost. This horse will lead in a group.

The confident, more experienced extroverted rider looking for endurance with a bit more excitement might select the *Talker.* This horse will give his heart and go all day. He is sure-footed and can go at speed. He will lead if the rider is confident and go as long as the rider wants. Just remember: this horse has lots of energy but often reacts more quickly when frightened.

HUMAN INTROVERT

There are two types of introverted humans: *Mediators* and *Analysts*.

Introverts tend to prefer a horse that will do the task fluidly but with less speed and more perfection. They like control—precision riding, for example. They want their horse to be proficient at lateral movement, stopping, backing-up, or "putting his nose" where asked.

Introverted riders are known to be very quiet with their body language, with quiet hands and not aggressive with their movement. Any horse they ride needs to be receptive to subtle body and leg cues.

Mediators like taking the time to make a horse perfect. You will see many of them at the show grounds: they enjoy grooming a horse to perfection and showing off their riding skills. You will find *Mediators* in dressage, Western pleasure, and trail classes.

Analysts like to "organize" with a horse. This may be related to breeding or keeping track of records. They are innovative people and enjoy riding through obstacles or trail-type competitions. Many trainers are *Analysts* as they enjoy figuring out what makes a horse work. You will see *Analysts* at handicapped "therapy" barns, as mounted police, or at ranch events.

Both *Analysts* and *Mediators* enjoy quiet time just grooming their horses. *Mediators* also like horses that show a lot of affection—they want a horse to love. *Analysts* might prefer a horse that comes when called because they want a horse that likes them but they also want that "level" of training.

The perfect horses for the *Analyst* are one of the two introverted types: either the *Thinker* (when the rider prefers a safer mount) or the *Actor* (when she wants a little more of a challenge or a horse that moves really well).

When an introverted person has less confidence, is a novice rider or has health issues, she might look for the *Thinker*. When trail riding, both enjoy taking things a bit more slowly: enjoying the scenery and riding in the middle of a group or alone. (The Extrovert may not be as comfortable with this horse because he can be "in-your-space" friendly, slower-paced and not like being in the lead position.)

A confident, more experienced Introvert

Looking to Purchase

When purchasing a new horse, there are a few rules of thumb. First, talk to the current owner. Tell her what you want to use this horse for in your life. See if she can tell you why this horse would work for you. However, don't rely on the word of the current owner alone. Ideally, you will take a trainer with you; if not, there are still some things you can do to help in the assessment.

We always recommend you make at least three visits to a prospective horse to view him at different times and in different scenarios: one in the morning with the horse in his stall, one at feeding time, and one when the horse is out in the pasture with buddies.

who wants precision might select an *Actor*. This horse, with a confident rider, will work hard to be perfect; he is normally very athletic but with less "go" than the *Talker*. When trail riding, if you enjoy a light-stepping horse that never touches a log or ground rail, and fluidly goes sideways, you will enjoy this horse. But remember, you need to be focused at all times with an *Actor* and realize that he can become unpredictable very easily—and very quickly.

HORSE EXTROVERT

As mentioned, when you are choosing a horse to trail ride all day; do endurance, cross-country, or eventing, you will need a more extroverted horse—a *Worker* or *Talker*. Here are some of the traits that are signs of this component, signs that you should look for when you first see the horse, perhaps to buy him. He:

- Will probably walk right up to you when you open the stall door, possibly getting "into your space" and appearing very interested in what you're doing.

- Will be "lively" when stepping out of the stall.

- Might be vocal about everything going on around him.

- Is often the first horse taken out to pasture as he does not have patience to wait.

- Will probably take off running when you turn him out. When he's in a playful mood, he's the horse that rears up, strikes at the others, and may even bite.

- Is often considered the herd leader.

- May be active in the stall or at the gate when it's feeding time.

- Doesn't stand still for very long.

HORSE INTROVERT

If you prefer slower, shorter trail rides, or want a horse for Western pleasure, roping, team penning, driving, or to use for therapy, you should look for the Introvert—a *Thinker* or *Actor*. (This horse is also good for short spurts of speed.) Use the same process of talking to the owner and observing the horse (see sidebar , p. 115). When you walk up to the stall door, you may notice some of the following traits:

The horse:
- Appears curious when you open the stall but may not approach you.

- Seems quiet.

- May look lazy.

- May be curious about how to do things such as untie the lead rope.

- Goes slowly, not pushing to be in front of you when you lead him.

- When turned out, once he is through the gate he will wait for an extra pat or rub, or just drop his head to eat where he stands.

- Stands quietly at feeding time as if he knows the grain will get there soon.

HORSE: RIGHT VS. LEFT BRAIN

Next, decide whether the horse is more right- or left-brained. Which to choose will depend on what you are confident with, what discipline you choose and your riding experience.

Right Brain Traits:

The horse:

- Can be overly alert (*RBE* and *RBI*).

- Can be quite vocal (*RBE*).

- Has white showing in the eyes (*RBE* and *RBI*).

- May rear (*RBE*).

- May stand off from the herd (*RBI*).

- May run or bolt (*RBE*).

- May be seen blowing or snorting *(RBE* and *RBI)*.

Visual Characteristics:

He may have one or more:

- Longer than normal nose and head that appears out of balance to his body.

- Distance between eyes to ears that is much shorter than eyes to nose.

- Small "pig eyes."

- Ears that are very close together, not lined up above the eyes but "inset" from them.

Like right-brained people, right-brained horses are based in emotion. Unfortunately, while such people tend to have more creativity, the right-brained horse tends to react more with fear. Some of this fear may be as a result of bad conformational traits. This horse normally goes into "flight" mode when stressed (the left-brained horse tends to go into "fight" mode.) Of course, not every horse with bad conformation is unpredictable. For all these reasons it's imperative that this horse has a good and patient trainer.

Be sure to check on your horse's breed standards as some horse breeds lend themselves to these characteristics, in which case they are not unusual.

Left Brain Traits:

The horse:

- Appears calm (*LBE* and *LBI*).

- Holds his head a bit lower. If he looks up at something, he easily lowers it again (*LBI*).

- Moves with purpose (*LBE*).

- Socializes in a group or herd. Usually likes to play with other horses (*LBE* and *LBI*).

- Plays face tag (*LBI*).

- Drives other horses *(LBE)*.

Visual characteristics:

He has:

- Eyes that are large and soft.

- Eyes to ears that are close to the same distance as eyes to nose.

- No white noticeable in the eyes.

- Ears wide-set aligned directly above eyes.

- Generally correct conformation: that is, not extreme in any one area.

(Review detailed information on physical conformation traits in chapter 7, p. 101.)

Left-brained people and horses are more "logical." In horses, this means they live life with more self-confidence and are generally calmer. When something goes wrong, the horse can think it through and deal with it much more quickly than the more right-brained horse.

Human and Horse: Comparison of Right- and Left-Brained Traits

HUMAN	HORSE
Right-brained people are creative, like to design.	Right-brained horses are impulsive.
Left-brained people are logical and enjoy science and math.	Left-brained horses are clever and want a purpose.
Introverted people get energy from being alone.	Introverted horses are quiet.
Extroverted people get energy from other people.	Extroverted horses don't like being held back.
Introverted people take a long time to make a final decision.	Introverted horses need to take their time on new tasks.
Extroverted people are high energy and enjoy activities with movement.	Extroverted horses like to move their feet.
Introverted people don't like loud places.	Introverted horses don't like loud people.
Introverted people like detailed activities.	Introverted horses like obstacles.
Extroverted people like to reach a goal.	Extroverted horses just want to go.

8.2

Matching the Right Job to the Right Horse

Here, we are offering a list of riding disciplines and activities for the horse personality best suited to the job. It is important to note that while *any* horse could perform *any* discipline, having the right personality for the job not only gives the horse a better chance at success, it also makes him happier. There would be fewer ring-sour horses seen at the various competitions if only the discipline matched the horse's personality style.

When selecting a horse for a specific discipline, you must first look at his body. A horse that doesn't have the right conformation for a sport will be unlikely to succeed at it no matter what his personality.

Bloodlines can also be important when you plan to compete. Once correct conformation and good bloodlines have been established, then you can look at the horse's personality. The best possible situation is when the horse and rider match each other's personalities *and* the horse personality is appropriate for the riding discipline.

Many competitions at shows lend themselves to a more right-brained horse. That's because such a horse needs to be happy being given a lot of direction and repetitions. The horse that gets bored easily, or doesn't like the rigors of doing the same thing over and over will not be as successful—or happy. The left-brained horse excels in areas with more variety and less intense direction. As with humans, in most cases, the best horses are those with more balanced scores in their questionnaire.

Also through an understanding of which horses excel in which disciplines, you are able to select other activities your horse might enjoy. Any horse can become bored spending years doing just one type of riding. With new options, you can give you and your horse a break and do something else you can both enjoy.

Please note that some events will work with more than one personality type. Additionally, the same discipline may have more than one application, and each application may take a different horse. For example: carriage driving may range from lovely rides in the countryside to competitive driving through obstacles. Each event requires a different kind of horse (figs. 8.2 & 8.3).

- CARRIAGE DRIVING (PLEASURE)—*Thinker.* For a leisurely drive in the country or a sleigh ride in the winter, this horse will be confident and prefers a slower, more enjoyable job.

- CARRIAGE DRIVING (COMPETITIVE)—*Worker.* This is a speed event where you want a faster moving yet left-brained horse.

- HALTER—*Actor.* You need a horse that can focus on the handler, keep his feet still, and look alert.

- COWBOY MOUNTED SHOOTING—*Thinker* or *Worker.* The horse needs to be quick and able to handle the rider shooting a gun.

- CUTTING—*Thinker.* This horse is judged on his ability to separate a single cow from a herd of cattle. The horse needs to be calm yet have quick movement.

- COMPETITIVE TRAIL—*Thinker.* Unlike endurance, factors other than overall time taken to complete the ride are considered. Some of these competitions are a judged trail ride, maneuvering through obstacles, while others are a form of "pace race" where the horse has a certain time to reach a designated point.

- DRESSAGE—*Actor* and *Talker.* The horse must respond smoothly and accurately to the rider's aids. Dressage requires a horse to respond to the rider's requests without question, so the right-brained horse is what is needed for this discipline.

- ENDURANCE—*Worker* and *Talker.* The Extrovert likes to go all day.

- EVENTING—*Worker* or *Talker.* This horse needs to be brave and have a good work ethic. But a too extreme *Worker* (meaning his left-brained scores are very high) will struggle with the dressage, and a too extreme *Talker* (right-brained scores are very high) will struggle with the crowds and cross-country. A high Extrovert score is good for eventing.

- GYMKHANA OR CONTESTING—*Talker* or *Thinker,* These events are about speed and maneuvering around obstacles such as cones, poles, and barrels. In good hands, the *Talker* will listen to the rider for direction yet give all the speed he has. A *Thinker* can do the quick bursts of speed needed for these arena competitions.

- HUNTER SEAT EQUITATION AND SHOW HUNTER—*Actor.* These events are judged on ability, cadence, and style, not on speed.

- SHOW JUMPING—*Talker* and *Worker.* The object of this sport is to jump a clear round and finish under the allotted time. Some events are judged against the clock in addition to jumping clear.

- LIBERTY HORSE—*Worker.* This event is done with no lines attached to the horse. It requires the horse to be confident and curious.

- RANCH SORTING OR TEAM PENNING—*Thinker* and *Worker.* These sports require two or three riders and horses on each team. The horses need to quietly cut up to three cows from a herd and drive them into a pen.

- REINING—*Actor.* In this Western sport where the horse performs the movements to set patterns, he needs to be responsive and in tune with his rider, whose aids should not be easily observed.

- SADDLE SEAT—*Talker.* The horse needs to be very energetic but still remain responsive to the rider's aids.

Social Styles Matching Specific Riding Activities

WORKER (LBE)	THINKER (LBI)	ACTOR (RBI)	TALKER (RBE)
Carriage Driving: Competitive	Carriage Driving: Pleasure	Conformation/Halter	Dressage
Cowboy Mounted Shooting	Competitive Trail	Dressage	Endurance
Endurance	Cowboy Mounted Shooting	Hunters	Eventing
Eventing	Cutting	Hunter Seat Equitation	Gymkhana/ Contesting
Jumper	Gymkhana/ Contesting	Reining	Reining
Liberty	Ranch Sorting	Halter	Saddle Seat
Ranch Sorting	Team Roping / Calf Roping	Showmanship	Jumper
Show Jumping	Team Penning	Trail Class	Trail Riding
Team Penning	Therapy Horse	Working Cow Horse	
Trail Riding	Trail Class	Western Pleasure	
Trick Training	Working Cow Horse	Working Horsemanship	
	Western Horsemanship		

8.3

- SHOWMANSHIP—*Actor.* This class is about maneuvering a horse in hand through a pattern or obstacles. The horse needs to be focused on his handler and know where to put his feet.

- TEAM ROPING AND CALF ROPING—*Thinker.* This event is about short bursts of speed, stopping, and holding a cow.

- THERAPY HORSE—*Thinker.* This personality is a good fit because therapy horses need to be calm around noises (prosthetics perhaps) and a lot of rider movement. The horse needs to be ready to stop his feet when needed.

- TRAIL CLASS—*Actor* and *Thinker.* The horse is required to be agile and have good manners.

- WESTERN PLEASURE—*Actor.* The sport judged by the horse's suitability for a relaxed but collected cadence with a relatively slow speed.

- WORKING COW HORSE—*Thinker.* This competition is judged on accuracy, timing, responsiveness, as well as how the horse moves into a herd and quietly cuts a single cow.

Note

There should be no shame in selling your horse when there isn't a good match. It is often better for both the horse and rider.

CHAPTER 9

Testing Our Matching Personality Theories

I N THIS CHAPTER, we'll tell you some stories based on real situations at three breeding farms, which are represented as Breeding Farm A, B, and C.

Visiting the farms was an excellent "test bed" for us in many ways. We were able to test our personality theory against many horses quickly, as well as look at the physical traits against breed standard to confirm our conformation thoughts. We also wanted to look at horse type vs. discipline and what personality types resulted from breeding which pairs.

Breeding Farm A

The first story is about a couple who breed, raise, and train racing Quarter Horses. They have been in business for a long time and over the years have become known for producing a very specific type of horse.

They have their own stallions onsite, but had recently lost their primary stallion of many years when we visited. They had replaced him with a new one at the beginning of the breeding season. The research we conducted consisted of foals from three onsite stallions and multiple onsite mares. The foals on the ground were all from the new stallion, his first for this farm.

The primary owner, (we'll call her "*Amanda Analyst*"), is an *Analyst/ Powerful*. She had very few *Mediator* or *Advocate* traits. On quick review, if she was a rider, her matching horse should be a *Thinker* or an *Actor*, but since she didn't ride, we found her best "matching" horse personalities were *Thinker* and *Worker*. Over the years, like all people with many horses, she had several she really liked, and a few she didn't care for so much. She also had a "best buddy" horse when growing up.

Our first test was to discuss all the horses with Amanda as a preliminary overview of their personality. Later, we went to the farm and met each horse in person to confirm his or her personality. What we found was that most of her mares were *Thinkers*. She had selected them first based on their bloodlines and conformation for speed. She also had a price range in mind, which fit her financial situation. When all things were equal, she would then pick the mares easiest to handle. She wanted them to be friendly and to like her.

If you review the traits of a *Thinker*, he is good at short bursts of speed, such as Quarter Horse racing (quarter of a mile), barrel racing, and roping. They are also great therapy horses as they are easy to handle and can even appear lazy. They are quiet and make great broodmares.

Interestingly enough, all three of Amanda's stallions were *Thinkers*, too. Despite this, however, Coax, her original stallion, displayed one set of traits, while Ben (her newest stallion) had almost a complete opposite set of traits— all within the same personality. Remember, we said when you look at the traits of any given human personality you will usually find that you don't possess all of them; the same is true of horses.

Coax was a *Thinker* of the calmest nature. As we reviewed his foals, we found, without exception, they were all Introverts. Coax was not really interested in the breeding process. He knew his job, but never got excited. In the charts on personalities, he fell under the "lazy, disinterested" traits.

Her second stallion, Thomas, was also a *Thinker* with a personality much like Coax, but not as calm.

Her new stallion, Ben, was a *Thinker,* as well. However, he was somewhat pushy—that is, defiant—and he got very excited during the breeding process with a tendency to charge. When not breeding, he was calm, clever, and enjoyed human involvement.

Had Amanda been interested in breeding for longer races, a *Thinker* would not have been the best choice. Short-distance racing is usually done by Quarter Horses while long-distance racing is for Thoroughbreds who are more extroverted and bred to have more endurance.

When Coax, a *Thinker*, was the primary stallion and he was bred to the mares, also for the most part *Thinkers*, the foals tended to have *Thinker* personalities.

With three new foals on the ground by Ben (a *Thinker*—a left-brained introvert with some extroverted traits) we found one of the three, Wilson, was much more active and didn't feel the need to stay close to his dam. Wilson was a *Thinker* but definitely displayed traits that could be considered almost extroverted. We are looking forward to his racing because we think the left-brained horse excelling at short bursts of speed, coupled with the extroverted trait of not wanting to keep his feet still, just might be the perfect racing Quarter Horse. These extroverted traits should keep him going full out to the finish line.

As a primary *Analyst* with a strong *Powerful* side, Amanda could actually pick either Introvert or Extrovert. On the other hand, Amanda had almost no right-brained traits. Additionally, as mentioned, Amanda didn't ride, so riding ability didn't play a role in selecting a left- or right-brained horse. All these circumstances made Amanda's "matching" horse a little more complicated, yet she was consistently drawn to a *Thinker* without even realizing it.

Through our conversations with her, we determined she didn't really care for the right-brained horses as much as she liked the left-brained ones. While she could deal with a few extroverted traits, she really didn't like either the *Actor* or the *Talker*. Looking at the core personalities, this confirms that a person solidly based in logic (left-brained) does not click with a horse that is more emotional (right-brained), but a balanced Introvert/Extrovert can work well with either.

To help confirm our conformation vs. personality theory, we did a field observation prior to discussing traits with the owner. When we first observed the foals in the field, Marry determined their personality by looking at eyes, ears, and conformation compared to the Quarter Horse breed standard. Later, the foals' actions confirmed she was correct in each one of her determinations.

While not discussed here, it also confirmed that early foal training had played a big role. Amanda imprints and handles her foals from day one. Being an equine vet, she is very aware of proper handling procedures and it shows quickly on the foals.

Study Sample

FOAL	MARE	STALLION
Vinny: Thinker (LBI)	Larky: Thinker (LBI)	Coax: Thinker (LBI)
Ernie: Actor (RBI)	Larky: Thinker (LBI)	Thomas: Thinker (LBI)
Lizzy: Worker (LBE)	Pumpkin: Talker (RBE)	Thomas: Thinker (LBI)
Rudy: Thinker (LBI)	Tango: Thinker (LBI)	Ben: Thinker (LBI)
Simon: Thinker (LBI)	Pumpkin: Talker (RBE)	Ben: Thinker (LBI)
Wilson: Thinker with many extrovert modifiers (LBI)	Mable: Talker (RBE)	Ben: Thinker (LBI)

9.1

This initial study was exciting because it confirmed every one of our theories:

- Human/horse attraction.

- Conformation/personality connection.

- Breeding personality theory.

- Discipline theory.

As of 2012, the three foals Rudy, Simon, and Wilson ran their first races. All three placed well, but Wilson won the first time out.

Breeding Farm B

The next farm we visited provided an incredible opportunity for our research. The owner, who we will call "*Diane Powerful*," is what we consider an "extreme" *Powerful* (had a very high core-personality score). Diane, whose matching horse (and favorite type of horse) is a *Worker* operates a breeding stable as well as two drill teams. Starting with her grandfather, this farm has bred and raised Mountain Pleasure horses from the same bloodlines for three generations.

Diane provides many of the horses for her drill teams, which are made up of people ranging from 12 to 20 years of age. Her daughter, an *Advocate* whose horse match is a *Talker*, also gives riding lessons on these same horses and she cheers the kids on to do well. (Interestingly, we have found many of the people who teach children to ride are *Advocates*.)

Diane's horses have to be able to handle all sorts of riders and activities. The same horse might be a trail horse one day, on the drill team the next, the show ring the next, a lesson horse by day, and in a parade that night. All this is done with riders who may or may not have riding experience. In some instances, Diane even uses young horses for these young people to ride. These horses have to do it all.

Over the past 20-plus years, Diane has selected the horses for her drill team riders and students as well as sold horses to a variety of new owners. In all the years she has been doing this, she said she has only had one owner return a horse because of a personality mismatch. When she was unable to provide a horse for any of the students, she helped them purchase the right horse elsewhere. We couldn't wait to ask her how she did it. Unfortunately, she said, "It was just intuition." However, after spending some time with her, we began to understand she instinctively knew an introverted child needed an introverted horse. Then the person's experience level and daredevil tendencies filled in the rest. This was the same for the extroverted child and horse.

We spent hours going over all the breeding pairs she had on the farm. We found she bred an Introvert to an Extrovert every time. This is what gave her the balance that allowed her to provide a horse for everyone who came through her gates. Almost without exception, her horses were well balanced and versatile.

We found another interesting detail while studying this group of horses. While breeding an Introvert to an Extrovert does give some of each, our research revealed the horse with the strongest traits in his or her particular personality usually produced more foals matching their personality. For example, Diane bred Keeper, an "extreme" *Talker (RBE)*, to Rennie, a *Thinker (LBI)* six times. Five of the six foals were Extroverts, matching their dam.

We really got lucky when we learned the drill team would be participating in a big event during our visit. Not only did we get to interview Diane, we were able to interview all the riders and evaluate their horses.

We hit the road to attend the big event. We spent an entire morning interviewing the drill team. They were an amazing bunch of young people ranging from 14 to 20 years of age. We were inclined to believe we would find most of them would be extroverted and probably right-brained. We felt this way because they loved the excitement of the drill team and rode a lot of Diane's *Talker* horses. However, we were a little surprised to find there was nearly an even split of personality types. While they enjoyed drill team, some actually preferred trail riding, or training and showing.

In two instances, we were concerned because the horse and rider personalities didn't match. After spending some time talking to these riders, we determined the horse each was riding that day was *not* their favorite horse. When we evaluated these riders another day on their favorite horse, we had a match. In every instance, the horse and rider personality fit perfectly.

Back at the farm the next day, we were able to observe riding lessons. This was another great opportunity to test our theory. We learned that even with a young child and young horse, horse and rider still needed to match personalities in order to be successful. We studied two eight-year-old new students. Jordan was an Extrovert and Shannon, an Introvert. Jordan and Shannon were both struggling with their assigned lesson horses: Jordan was on Fanny, an Introvert, and Shannon was riding Jezzy, an Extrovert.

We watched as Fanny pinned her ears and hunched her back up making a very uncomfortable and worrisome ride for Jordan. Shannon, riding Jezzy, was losing confidence quickly as Jezzy tossed her head and wanted to move faster than Shannon wanted to go. The instructor brought them in and switched horses and riders. It was interesting to see how Jezzy stopped tossing her head and was moving at a speed that Jordan liked. Fanny had her ears up and remained calm while Shannon enjoyed the slower paced ride around the arena.

We can't thank Diane and all the riders enough for spending hours with us to further our research.

Breeding Farm C

Finally, we interviewed *"**Anna Beth Mediator**."* She started by breeding Western pleasure Quarter Horses—all ***Actors*** *(RBI)*. This was not only a discipline she enjoyed but also the personality to which she was drawn (Introvert to Introvert). As she became a more experienced rider, she went into reining. Fortunately, reining also required an ***Actor***. Since Anna Beth was an experienced rider with years of training and breeding, she was comfortable and liked doing what matched her own and her horse's personality.

Over the years she expanded her training, reining, and showing career and eliminated the breeding farm. She is now a trail class judge, active in the reining circuit, and an equine chiropractor. While her favorite horse is still an ***Actor***, should she ever make the decision to move away from the Western pleasure discipline and need to select horses that are not her perfect match, her knowledge and self-confidence would now allow her to deal with any horse's personality style she may encounter.

CHAPTER 10

Personality Matching: Brief Summary

B efore we move on to the training section of this book that starts on page 181, we'll briefly summarize the information about personality matching in human and horse. Then to support the information, we introduce five imaginary people—in "real-life" settings—and discuss their quest for a horse. So let's recap the theories presented so far in this book.

Personality Analysis: Human and Horse

In a perfect world, there would be only four types of people and horses, and they would never change (figs. 10.1 and 10.2). Of course, you now know that isn't true. Most people and many horses have mod-

HUMAN	HORSE
Analyst (LBI)	*Thinker* (LBI)
Powerful (LBE)	*Worker* (LBE)
Mediator (RBI)	*Actor* (RBI)
Advocate (RBE)	*Talker* (RBE)

10.1

ifying characteristics. In all cases, a significant emotional event can change personality traits.

So if you put this together to match core personality Social Styles (assuming all are experienced or confident riders), you have:

| **Human** | *Analyst* (LBI) | **Horse** | *Thinker* (LBI) |
| | Detailed | | Clever |

Both "want" to go slowly.

| **Human** | *Powerful* (LBE) | **Horse** | *Worker* (LBE) |
| | Leader | | Confident |

Both "want" to keep moving.

| **Human** | *Mediator* (RBI) | **Horse** | *Actor* (RBI) |
| | Amiable | | Faithful |

Both "need" reassurance.

| **Human** | *Advocate* (RBE) | **Horse** | *Talker* (RBE) |
| | Expressive | | Flighty |

Both move out of "need."

Since we don't live in a perfect world and very few humans or horses fall perfectly into just one personality, we must consider a variety of traits from many personalities. The traits that fall outside our *core* personality are called "modifiers." Humans and horses may start out with a "pure" core personality but it isn't long before modifiers start the personality-change process. There are many things that cause us to take on traits from the other personalities. Some are permanent changes and some are short-term.

Summary of Left/Right Brain and Introvert/Extrovert

HUMAN	HORSE
Left Brain: Reactions are based on logic.	Left Brain: Reactions are based on confidence.
Right Brain: Reactions are based on emotion.	Right Brain: Reactions are based on fear.
Introvert: Quiet; draws energy from within.	Introvert: Can't deal with loud sounds; likes standing still.
Extrovert: Outgoing; draws energy from a crowd.	Extrovert: Energetic; needs to keep moving.

10.2

HUMAN

Referred to as the "Z" Pattern, people can "Z" through their personalities daily (see p. 15). Under stress, humans cross the Introvert/Extrovert boundary line first because it's easiest to move from "ask" to "tell" or "tell" to "ask."

Then, when more stress is encountered, the "Z" moves across the Left Brain/Right Brain line, the "logical" and "emotional" boundary. To give you an example: a *Powerful (LBE)* would first become an *Analyst (LBI)*, then an *Advocate (RBE)*, and finally a *Mediator (RBI)*. An extroverted, logical person first moves to being an introverted logical person; then to being an extroverted emotional person; and, finally, to an introverted emotional person.

This is usually a temporary situation that can develop quickly and leave quickly. However, a significant emotional event such as a loss of a job, death of a family member, or divorce can drive a person to becoming another personality for an extended period—even permanently. These types of life-changing events can result in a person changing to any of the four core personalities, which can remain her new core until something new causes a change.

HORSE

In our domesticated horse world, training can make a huge difference as a modifier, as can significant emotional events such as abuse. The old saying, "He just needs a lot of wet saddle pads," can also hold some truth as a modifier. While good training can give a horse the appearance of taking on a few traits that cross the Introvert/Extrovert boundary, just remember that except in cases of abuse, horses rarely cross that boundary. This means the horse that "needs" to move his feet will *always* need to move them, and the horse that doesn't, *never* will.

On the other hand, training often helps balance a right-brained (flighty) horse with more left-brained (confident) tendencies. Knowing how to "read" a horse, to determine if his problem is caused by his personality, abuse, bad training, or pain is critical to giving him both physical and mental balance.

Personality changes in horses tend to be long-term. Just remember, when selecting a horse, if things go really badly, a horse *will* revert to his core personality. If you decide to choose a horse outside your personality match, be sure you can live with his core personality reactions.

· · · · · · · · ·

Five Case Studies

You are about to meet five horse owners (not real people) who have different reasons for wanting a horse, for varying uses, and learn how they find the animal they want. In some cases, we have selected the perfect horse, and for others we gave them what you might *think* would have been the perfect horse, then explain how and why he didn't work out. These short stories will give you a better understanding of basic personalities of both humans and horses and how these interact. You will also be introduced to the concept of personality vs. discipline (or "job") for the horse.

Donna

IDENTIFYING DONNA'S SOCIAL STYLE

When Donna took her Social Style Questionnaire her scores were: *Analyst* 12, *Powerful* 18, *Mediator* 2, *Advocate* 8, **Left Brain 30, Right Brain 10, Extrovert 26, Introvert 14.**

What does this tell us about Donna? First of all, with a total score of 30 out of 40 in the left-brained half of the Social Style Grid, she is very left-brained. Next, you see that her Extrovert score, totaling 26, is much higher than her Introvert score of only 14. Finally, her top score is *Powerful*, which further confirms she is definitely *LBE*.

Judging from her Social Style of *Powerful*, Donna might be impatient, abrupt, goal-oriented, forward-thinking, and driven. She is likely to make decisions quickly, tell people what to do, and doesn't require—or like—a lot of detail.

As her strongest modifier is *Analyst*, she might also be logical, detailed, methodical, and pensive. She might have trouble making decisions, excessively analyze things, and conduct her own research.

Lastly, her *Advocate* side could kick in providing some of the following attributes: dramatic, artsy, creative, high energy, and overly enthusiastic with little regard for time schedules. Additionally, she could have the ability to see the "big" picture and be the cheerleader.

On the other hand, since Donna's score as *Mediator* is so low, few if any of those traits would be exhibited.

MEET DONNA

She is 5 feet, 2 inches tall and near retirement age. She has been in top management for many years. She enjoys being with people and is very comfortable speaking in front of large groups. However, Donna is sometimes viewed by others as abrupt and impatient. She sees the big picture and sets long-term goals for her organization quite easily. She pays close attention to detail because her job requires it, but really doesn't enjoy all those facts. She is energetic and makes decisions quickly. She is driven to meet deadlines, and strives for perfection. In fact, this need to keep "doing" often makes it difficult for her to just sit and chat, or relax and watch TV. Donna is happiest when she is moving around, planning and organizing.

HORSE SEARCH

Donna is looking forward to retirement and a chance to start riding that horse she has always wanted. While she has never really ridden a horse except for a few nose-to-tail trail rides as a child, her dream has always been to own a horse and trail ride in every state in the US. Long rides down new trails are just what she needs when she stops working.

After several conversations with friends who ride and extensive Internet research, she has decided she wants a small, gaited horse. So back to the Internet she goes. Looking through the several pages of gaited horses, Donna finds a few she thinks are very pretty. Donna has been striving for project perfection her entire life, so pretty is important to her. She decides a Palomino will fill the bill perfectly. She especially likes the dark ones with white tails and manes.

Donna also has a price range. Between size, price range, how far she is willing to travel to get the horse, and "being pretty," she first narrowed it down to about 15 horses.

But Donna needs to consider the fact she is a novice rider and a friend told her a gelding would be her best bet. That narrowed the list down to 10 horses to choose from.

Another friend told her she needed a calm horse, at least eight years old, and with trail experience. Now the list is narrowed down to five. She calls each owner and tells them what she wants to do with the horse. Based on those calls, she decides "Hawk" is the right horse for her. Hawk is quiet, slow, and steady. He has been trail ridden in many states, never spooks, and is calm and has a good "whoa." He stands quietly for mounting and dismounting and has passed his vet check.

So Donna is off to meet Hawk. Because Donna makes decisions quickly, one look at that 14.2-hand, dark Palomino with his long flowing tail and mane was all it took. She knew that not only was he quiet and calm, he would also draw looks from everyone they passed. Hawk went home with her that very day.

THE HORSE CONNECTION

Donna takes a few riding lessons. They last about 45 minutes and all she really wants to learn is the basics—start, stop, and steer. By the time her retirement date arrives, Donna is ready to hit the trails with a few close friends and Hawk. Yes, indeed, Hawk is not only beautiful, but for those short beginning trail rides, he is great.

Based on what you have read so far, is this the horse you would have picked for Donna? Well let's see how her purchase worked out over time.

THE HORSE

Let's see how Hawk would score on his questionnaire: *Thinker* 19; *Actor* 5, **Introvert 20, Extrovert 4, Left Brain 21, Right Brain 3.**

The *Thinker* is an LBI. That makes him clever, defiant, food-oriented, careful with novice riders, and prone to being stubborn. The *Actor* modifier is an RBI. That makes him quiet, obedient, intense, not able to trust, and sometimes unpredictable. When he does trust his rider, he can be precise in his movements. Notice the personality modifier is still within the Introvert personality. (As we've said, unlike humans, horses rarely cross over the Introvert/Extrovert boundary, but on the other hand, they do cross over Right Brain/Left Brain boundary.)

Hawk sounds like the perfect horse for a beginning rider, and, for many people, he would be perfect. Hawk is a very clever horse. Some people would call him lazy, maybe even dull. He doesn't shy away at anything; he is "Steady Eddy." However, Hawk doesn't like to "go" all day: he is good for a short ride, one to two hours, then he is mentally ready for a break. This should be a nice long break, with some fresh hay, a drink of water, and a snooze.

THE OUTCOME

This works out perfectly when Donna first begins riding because she isn't in shape to ride for any longer than about two hours.

The first several rides go well and build Donna's confidence. However, in a few months, her core personality surfaces and she finds when she is out with her friends, she would like to lead the group, go at a faster pace, and take longer rides. The fun in trail riding for her is to "ride," not stop for long rests or breaks.

Donna is getting a little weary of Hawk acting tired when she thinks he should be in shape by now and should be able to handle the fast pace and longer rides. At the same time, Hawk is getting tired of Donna always pushing him to do more. He begins pushing back. While many actions can be trained out of horses, most horses will eventually revert to their core personality.

A *Thinker* like Hawk may buck when pushed, which is exactly what happens on one of the rides. Then, when they get back to the camp and Donna ties him to the rail, he pushes into Donna using his head. Not being a trainer or or very horse savvy, she doesn't pick up on the signals Hawk is sending her. Stress starts to build up.

Donna is quickly learning her beautiful perfect trail horse is not working out for her as well as she thought he would. But, he is still that eight-year-old, "experienced trail gelding who doesn't spook and has been ridden all over the place" that will stand perfectly for the novice to mount and dismount. So what happened?

COMPARING RIDER AND HORSE

The same trait that makes Hawk happy to stand for mounting and dismounting also makes him happy to stand for other reasons or even no reason. Hawk is a *Thinker* and Donna is a *Powerful*. Donna wants to "go, go, go" and wants her horse to "go, go, go" as well for as long as she desires without question or hesitation.

Hawk's personality:
- Wants to stand and think about things.
- Wants to stay with a group of horses.
- Likes to go for shorter rides.
- Enjoys eating.

Donna's personality:
- Does things with energy.
- Expects obedience without question.
- Focuses on the goal (or destination).
- Makes her the leader.

Is there a perfect "buddy" for Donna that will get her through the novice phase and still meet her long-term requirements? Yes, of course there is. She needs to look for a *Worker (LBE)* who has been through enough training for a novice. With a *Worker*, when Donna is ready to ask for more, her mount is also ready, willing, and happy to give it.

In summary, Donna is a *Powerful (LBE)* person mismatched to a *Thinker (LBI)* horse. The key mismatch is Extrovert to Introvert. By matching Extrovert to Extrovert, the goal-oriented and energetic person gets together with the faster I-want-to-move-my-feet horse.

In addition, given her level of experience and her age, Donna should be looking for a left-brained horse, one more apt to just move past anything scary rather than just react on emotion. Of course, a well-trained horse is an absolute necessity for any beginner.

WHAT HAPPENED TO DONNA?

If Donna had gone into the purchase with the goal of building her riding confidence, Hawk might have been a great starter horse for her because a *Thinker* is often called the "Steady Eddy" of the horse world. In that case, she would have planned to sell him (or keep him as a pet) and switch to an extroverted horse within a few months. However, most people don't want to buy and sell horses that often or keep them as yard ornaments. Fortunately, in this case, Donna was smart enough to realize the match wasn't right and this allowed Hawk to find his perfect owner.

Donna decides to talk to the local trainer and let him help her find the "perfect" horse this time. After watching her attending a few clinics and riding several of his horses, the trainer now understands her needs, and with careful consideration, he recommends a little red roan named Honey.

THE NEW HORSE

How did Honey score on her questionnaire?

Honey scored 20 points in the *Worker* and 4 points in the *Talker* categories (Extrovert 22, Introvert 2, Left Brain 20, Right Brain 4). This makes Honey a *Worker* with *Talker* modifiers. The *Worker* is an *LBE,* a horse that is friendly, mouthy, willful, and pushy but who will gladly work all day and is very confident with a novice rider.

The *Talker* is an *RBE.* The *Talker* modifiers may add traits like being vocal, impulsive, hyper-alert, and high-headed, but when Honey trusts her rider she will go anywhere.

The *Worker* trait gives her both the endurance and speed Donna wants as well as self-confidence, which helps a novice rider who doesn't want to risk getting hurt. Here is a horse ready to go—a no-nonsense type—just the horse needed for someone used to giving people instruction and expecting the job to get done.

WHAT HAPPENED TO HAWK?

Donna's willingness to find Hawk a new home paid off for both horse and rider. It wasn't long before a man named Jim contacted Donna about Hawk (see next story).

Jim

IDENTIFYING JIM'S SOCIAL STYLE

When Jim took his Social Style Questionnaire his scores were as follows: *Analyst* 17, *Powerful* 5, *Mediator* 6, *Advocate* 12, **Left Brain 22, Right Brain 18, Introvert 23, Extrovert 17.**

What does this tell us about Jim? First he is more left-brained with a total score of 22. He is more introverted with a score 23. Last, his highest Social Style score is in the *Analyst* quadrant and his highest modifier is *Advocate*.

His *Analyst* traits include being pensive, logical, intuitive, detailed, and methodical; however, he has a tendency to have trouble making decisions and analyzes things to death.

His *Advocate* side could kick in providing some of these attributes: dramatic, artsy, creative, high energy, flexible, overly enthusiastic, and with little regard for time schedules. Additionally, he has the ability to see the big picture and be the cheerleader. Because his scores are low in the other two Social Styles, he might not display any of their related traits.

MEET JIM

Jim is 5 feet, 10 inches tall, 35 years old and lives in Michigan. Jim is intuitive, logical, flexible, and sees the world as a whole. These traits along with his enjoyment of working alone or in small groups, drawing his energy from within, and being a good planner and problem solver, make him a good mounted police officer. His *Advocate* side needs some excitement, which he got from his hobby of roping cattle. His innate ability to build deep and strong friendships provided the human/horse bonding Hawk needed.

HORSE CONNECTION

Jim's an experienced rider who knows how to "read" horses. He is an *Analyst* *(LBI)* with *Advocate* *(RBE)* modifiers. Because he scores fairly evenly between Right and Left Brain as well as Introvert and Extrovert, he has a balanced personality. This makes it easy for him to align naturally. He understands Hawk.

His job is being a mounted police officer and Jim expects a lot from his horse. He works hard, and needs a horse to do not just one job, but several.

It takes a special kind of horse to "work" on the streets. Jim's current police horse was due to retire and he needed a replacement horse. Having seen what type of horse worked well for police work, he knew immediately Hawk would be a good candidate. Hawk passed all the entry tests with flying colors and soon became a working police horse.

THE OUTCOME

One day while out on patrol, Jim caught sight of a robber leaving a store and called for backup. Sirens were blaring as the police chased the robber around a building right into a parade going down Main Street. To the police in their cars, the vehicle chase was over. But Jim and Hawk maneuvered down the side of the parade, weaving in and out of all the people standing on the sidewalks. This allowed Jim to pursue the robber while the onlookers just thought he was part of the parade. Soon, Jim and Hawk walked right up next to the robber—he was walking in the parade as if he belonged there—stepped in front of him, and abruptly stopped. Jim then jumped off, arrested the man, and took him out to the police car. Meanwhile Hawk was perfectly content to stand quietly and wait for Jim's return.

After a hard day's work, Jim still found time to groom Hawk and give him plenty of hay before leaving. On weekends, Hawk and Jim liked to go to the arena and work on the obstacle course. Jim and Hawk participated in the obstacle course in the North American Police Equestrian Championships. Hawk loved the events and did very well. Of course, Hawk also greatly enjoyed the great "rubs" he got from Jim for a job well done. Now Hawk was ready for a long nap. This was the perfect situation for a *Thinker* horse.

Ellen

IDENTIFYING ELLEN'S SOCIAL STYLE

When Ellen took her Social Style Questionnaire her scores were as follows: *Analyst* **3**, *Powerful* **9**, *Mediator* **10**, *Advocate* **18**, **Left Brain 12, Right Brain 28, Introvert 13, Extrovert 27.**

What does this tell us about Ellen? First of all, with a total score of 28 out of 40 in the emotion/creative half of the Social Style Grid, this tells us she is right-brained. We then see her Extrovert score, totaling 27, is much higher than her Introvert score of only 13. Finally, her top score is *Advocate*, further confirming she is definitely *RBE*. By Social Style, Ellen is intuitive, enthusiastic, a "cheerleader," and self-confident, with a dry wit and a love for trivia. She hates detail unless it pertains to something that really interests her. She loves music and art and often volunteers for charity work.

She loves people, is very friendly and loves working in groups. However, she has a tendency to not focus completely on the job at hand, flitting from task to task and often wanting to be the center of attention. Her friends complain she is rarely on time for anything.

As Ellen's strongest modifier is *Mediator,* she may also be accommodating, friendly, and a great event planner. Her *Powerful* side could kick in providing some of the following attributes: impatience, being abrupt, goal-oriented, forward-thinking, and driven. However, since Ellen's score as *Analyst* is so low, few (if any) of those traits would be exhibited.

MEET ELLEN

Ellen is 5 feet, 8 inches tall. She was a cheerleader in high school and college. She majored in interior design but married right out of college and is now a stay-at-home wife and mother. For the first time, all her children are in school and she has some time to herself. She is finally getting to a point in her life where she can get the horse she has always wanted. As a child her cousin owned several horses and she had ridden frequently. Racing through the woods was her favorite part. (People who love the "thrill" of riding are often *Advocates*.)

HORSE SEARCH

With the children in school, she has some free time on her hands and can't wait to find her new perfect equine friend. Remembering how much she loved long rides and racing down the trails at top speed as a child, she knows what she wants to do with her horse. However, since she never actually owned a horse, she knows she needs to do some research before her purchase. Because she is so excited about the topic, she is willing to do some work before selecting and buying her own horse. Her research indicates she should buy a gaited horse.

Ellen reads that Mountain Pleasure horses are supposed to be fast and smooth, have endurance, and be very versatile. It sounds like this breed might be just the right horse for her. Since her children come home from school in the afternoon Ellen isn't interested in going on long rides just yet—just fast ones. However, she knows one day she will look forward to all-day rides again.

Ellen is now ready to begin her search. Because she makes decisions best when with a group of friends, the first thing she does is to get her future riding buddies together and discuss what horse she might like to own. They look at many websites and scan page after page. After selecting several options, including all colors and sizes, she decides she needs an "expert" opinion to help with the final decision. Ellen makes decisions easily and quickly but she also values outside input. She calls her cousin and gets the name of a good trainer in her area to help her find her perfect horse.

THE HORSE CONNECTION

This trainer understood that not every horse is for every person or for every type of riding. She also understood that while Ellen hadn't ridden for several years, she was an experienced rider with little fear and a lot of confidence. The trainer helped her select three horses she felt might work. Ellen and her trainer went to observe each of the three horses multiple times. Along with riding the horses, they also watched how they interacted with the other horses in a herd in the pasture, in the stalls and at feeding time. The trainer selected a 16-hand, 8-year-old, Mountain Pleasure Horse, named Sugar, with a conformation that would hold up to the speed and hours under saddle that Ellen wanted.

Through training, Sugar was confident enough to stand still for Ellen to mount and dismount. She stood quietly until Ellen was ready to go, but as soon as it was time, Sugar would move her feet. As Sugar had an excellent trainer, she had learned to trust humans and overcome her fears. She was now an emotionally balanced horse. While Sugar still had a tendency to be high-headed, Ellen was not concerned.

Because Ellen needed to board Sugar anyway, she felt the trainer's barn would be a great place to start. While not as close to her home as other barns, she knew initially having a trainer involved would be an important step. As soon as she brought Sugar home, she started working with the trainer to brush up on her skills and help her understand and utilize the appropriate cues for her new horse. An added bonus for Ellen was the trail system the trainer had through the woods right behind his stables.

THE HORSE

Let's see how Sugar did on her questionnaire.

She scored 13 as a *Worker* and 11 as a *Talker.* Then: Extrovert 22, Introvert 2, Left Brain 14, and Right Brain 10.

The *Worker* is an *LBE*. This makes Sugar confident with a novice rider, friendly, and willing to go all day. However, this also makes her willful and pushy. The *Talker* modifier is an *RBE*. This makes her impulsive and, at times, high-headed but willing to go anywhere her rider wants to go.

Sugar had lots of trail experience. Because she has several *Talker* points, it is possible she was more right-brained as a youngster, but lots of wet saddle pads and a good solid training program have made her well balanced (left-brained). Sugar still has the need to move her feet but she has learned to stand patiently while Ellen mounts. She loves to run at full speed for long distances but will slow and whoa easily and rarely spooks. On top of all that she is very pretty and loves attention. Sugar is actually a very well balanced *Worker*.

THE OUTCOME

Ellen had only "dreamed" of flying across the field on a horse. She hadn't actually tried riding at a fast speed since she was a child. However, she had the personality that indicated, given some time, she and her horse could fulfill her dream. The *Worker* type horse not only has the ability to run across country, but also has the personality to take some responsibility for speed and direction.

Both Ellen and Sugar's personalities liked speed; however, because Sugar was a *Worker*, a bit older and well trained, she could control her emotions quite well—even when moving very fast. Sugar quickly learned to read Ellen's body language and understand her cues; they became a team and best of friends.

COMPARING RIDER AND HORSE

You may be wondering why the trainer picked a *Worker* (*LBE*) horse for an *Advocate* (*RBE*) human. A very important part of a trainer's job is to understand and match the experience level of the human with the correct horse.

Based on personality, Ellen's direct match would have been a *Talker (RBE)*. Because Ellen hadn't ridden for several years, the **Worker** was a better match. The **Worker** allowed Ellen some time to get back in the swing of things and would still be the right horse when she is again an accomplished rider. During that initial period, the *Talker* might have become stressed and reacted accordingly to a lack of leadership skills.

Additionally, **Advocates** often use a lot of body language, which, in turn, can make a *Talker* nervous. As you can see the trainer matched an Extrovert to Extrovert. However, he selected a left-brained (meaning calmer) horse for a right-brained person because he felt it would give Ellen time to get reacquainted with her riding skills. Note: the horse's scores for Right and Left Brain were pretty close. Therefore, Sugar should provide for both current and future needs of her rider.

Sugar's personality:
- Keeps her feet moving.
- Wants to work all day.
- Doesn't spook easily.
- Feels confident with a novice rider.

Ellen's personality:
- Does things with energy.
- Enjoys the thrill of speed.
- Wants to go long distances.
- Can be the leader her horse needs.

This was a perfect match for Ellen. She was wise to go to a trainer who understood matching horse and rider for both her present situation as a novice rider and where she wanted to be in the future when she got more experience.

Andrew

IDENTIFYING ANDREW'S SOCIAL STYLE

When Andrew took his Social Style questionnaire his scores were as follows: *Analyst* **24**, *Powerful* **9**, *Mediator* **6**, *Advocate* **1**, **Left Brain 33**, **Right Brain 7**, **Introvert 30**, **Extrovert 10**.

What does this tell us about Andrew? First of all, with a total score of 33 out of 40 in the logical/thought half of the Social Style Grid, it tells us he is very left-brained. Next you see his Introvert score, totaling 30, is much higher than his Extrovert score of only 10. Finally, his top score is *Analyst*, which further confirms he is definitely a left-brained Introvert. From his Social Style, Andrew is pensive, logical, detailed, and methodical. As his strongest modifier is *Powerful*, he might also be impatient, abrupt, goal-oriented, forward-thinking, and driven. However, since both other scores are low Andrew probably shows very few traits from either *Mediator* or *Advocate*.

Andrew loves to research almost any topic, is quiet, and prefers to spend time alone or with a close friend or two. Andrew doesn't make friends easily but when he forms a friendship it is a deep and lasting one. He's good at small talk but doesn't really enjoy it. Andrew loves to do research and usually takes a long time to make a final decision. He fears he may have missed something or a better product will come along right after he makes his purchase. His ability to do tasks in order, be goal-oriented, know and follow rules, make master schedules, and view things from the parts to the whole makes Andrew an excellent programmer.

MEET ANDREW

Andrew is 6 feet, 2 inches tall. He is a middle-aged computer programmer and spends a lot of time on the details. He loves his job and has no desire to move into management. He and his wife have a very small circle of close friends and don't enjoy a lot of social events. He has decided that he would like to spend his free time with a horse.

As a child he rode in local horse shows, as an adult he has studied dressage and taken lessons. He loves the detailed precision necessary in both horse and rider. Andrew decided if the time and money were ever available, he would own a dressage horse.

As an *Analyst*, Andrew is most productive when he is alone in a quiet place, so he thought it might be fun to work one on one with his horse and his personality makes it possible for him to work with precision. Of course, it would take research and a deep understanding of the process.

HORSE SEARCH

Andrew, unlike many people, doesn't want someone else to help him select his horse. He wants to do some serious research on his own. He starts by making a list of all the things that need to be done before, during, and after his purchase. This includes everything from buying supplies, to building the fences and barn, to the first ride. Nothing will be left out. He will enjoy checking them off one by one as each task is completed to his satisfaction.

Next he puts together a spreadsheet of all the things he wants to evaluate in a horse. With spreadsheet in hand, he knows he wants a horse that is athletic enough to do dressage He is looking for size as his frame requires something taller, and he wants a horse that moves well with plenty of impulsion from behind. He also puts statistics into his spreadsheet about how well horses' bloodlines have performed in competition. He will also add information about whether or not the horse hauls well, and how he behaves when being clipped and handled. There is even a spot for details from a vet check.

The list of his requirements continues, but finally, after much consideration, Andrew identifies the type of horse he wants to buy. He knows correct conformation and abilities are needed to perform well.

On his spreadsheet of things to look for are:

- Clean gaits.
- Ability to be collected.
- Willingness to focus and go forward.
- Freedom of movement.
- Calm mind but curious.

It takes Andrew almost a year of research to select his horse; but that's okay because he enjoys the research almost as much as he will enjoy the purchase. With his spreadsheet in hand he has mapped all possible candidates with pros and cons. Today is the big day. He is going to pick up his new horse, Asher, a Dutch Warmblood

THE HORSE CONNECTION

To be absolutely sure of his decision, he has gone to visit Asher several times and has ridden him often.

The first time Andrew went to see Asher, he stood in his stall watching him approach. He was a quiet horse but he would normally pin his ears back when someone he didn't know walked up to him. It wasn't that he was mean, he just didn't trust people. He had gone through several owners and these experiences had magnified his distrust. Asher needed someone to make him feel safe.

Before Asher's current owner (an *Advocate*) purchased him, she had watched him being ridden several times. He seemed like a quiet, sensible horse. Because she had very little riding experience, she only rode him once in the arena before buying him. This lack of experience and confidence—and personality mismatch—was Asher's undoing. An *Advocate* tends to be impatient and just wants a horse to go. Her lack of experience needed a horse that behaved well and didn't spook easily. She was not someone who wanted to worry about comforting her horse. The more she rode him, the worse the partnership became. Things started to fall apart during one trail ride when a very large deer spooked him. Without an experienced rider to make him feel secure, he froze, then spun trying to get away. After this, his owner began to trust him less and became more nervous with each ride. Asher in return became more unpredictable. He finally came to the point of being so nervous that he would randomly shake, kick, bolt, and spin. Needless to say, his owner decided it was time to sell him.

Given this history, is this the horse you would even consider for Andrew? Andrew is an *Analyst (LBI)*. Asher is an *Actor (RBI)*.

THE HORSE

My guess is you are saying, "No," but Asher was actually perfect for Andrew. Before we look at Asher's scores we need to point out that Andrew had actually been aware of Asher for some time. He had in fact wanted to buy him when he was first for sale. He knew something about horse personalities and saw the potential in Asher. As he watched Asher go from quiet and calm to unpredictable, Andrew was sorry he hadn't purchased him. Needless to say, when Asher came up for sale again, Andrew couldn't wait to buy him.

Let's see how Asher scored on his questionnaire.

He scored 21 as an *Actor,* and 2 as a *Thinker,* and 1 as a *Talker*. Introvert score is 23, Extrovert 1, Right Brain 22, and Left Brain 2.

The *Actor* is an *RBI*. This makes him quiet, obedient, intense, and precise when he trusts his rider, but also unpredictable when he doesn't. With so few points in the *Thinker* category, you probably won't see many of those traits. (As I've mentioned, unlike humans, horses rarely cross the Introvert/Extrovert boundary.)

Asher is a seven-year-old Warmblood, very athletic, conformationally correct, and nice looking. He has large brown eyes and is quiet when he feels safe. Despite his lack of confidence, with an experienced rider who is patient and kind, Asher will be a wonderful dressage prospect. That rider is Andrew.

THE OUTCOME

Asher made an excellent dressage horse. In addition, it turned out that he had jumping ability so could also compete as a hunter.

Andrew was an experienced rider who chose a discipline that took both time and patience to achieve. Andrew didn't mind that Asher could be a little flighty. Andrew enjoyed spending quiet time and working on Asher's confidence. He was happy to spend hours on groundwork. He was an excellent complement to a horse that reacted from a fear-based perspective. They were indeed a perfect match. Asher finally had a place to feel safe and secure and took Andrew to first place often.

COMPARING RIDER AND HORSE

While the Introvert part is a match between horse and rider, once again you see a crossover between left-brained and right-brained. In this case, Andrew was an experienced rider with a lot of patience. For a right-brained horse like Asher with few left-brain modifiers, Andrew worked out well.

Actually, Andrew could have chosen either a *Thinker* (LBI) or an *Actor* (RBI). The determining factor for Andrew was the discipline he planned to enjoy with this horse. Horses with specific personalities not only excel in a certain discipline or job but also enjoy it. While Andrew is a *LBI*, he is willing to modify his personality slightly to work with a horse that will excel in the discipline he is interested in pursuing. The *Actor* with proper conformation is well suited for trail class, hunter, and dressage.

Asher needed someone to make him feel safe, to give him leadership with a soft but confident voice. He liked to take things slow. If he trusted you, he would be very obedient. He would place his feet exactly where told. If you would wait for him to understand, give him time to think, give an occasional treat and be gentle with him, he would do anything you asked of him.

Asher's personality:
- Can freeze, then react unpredictably when in fear.
- Is precise if he trusts his rider.
- Will focus.
- Is obedient.

Andrew's personality:
- Is detailed and precise.
- Is patient and willing to take things slow.
- Doesn't mind taking small steps toward a goal.
- Is very logical and focused.

This is a perfect match for Andrew. Together they became an award-winning team.

Annie

IDENTIFYING ANNIE'S SOCIAL STYLE

When Annie took her Social Style Questionnaire her scores were as follows: *Analyst* 6, *Powerful* 3, *Mediator* 21, *Advocate* 10, **Right Brain** 31, **Left Brain 9, Introvert 27, Extrovert 13.**

What does this tell us about Annie? First of all, with a total score of 31 out of 40 in the emotional/creative half of the Social Style Grid, it tells us she is very right-brained. Next we see Annie's Introvert scores, totaling 27, are much higher than her Extrovert scores of only 13. Finally, her top score is *Mediator*, which further confirms she is definitely *RBI*.

By Social Style, Annie is probably accommodating, friendly, loyal, and compliant. She enjoys being part of the team but sometimes has trouble saying "no." As her strongest modifier is *Advocate*, she might also be overly enthusiastic, dramatic, and artsy, with a lot of energy. She can also be the cheerleader of the group. Last of all, her *Analyst* side may kick in providing some of the following attributes: logical, detailed, and methodical. However, since Annie's score as *Powerful* is extremely low, few if any of those traits would be exhibited.

She is very compassionate, sometimes too much so. Annie can sit and chat about anything or nothing for hours with her friends (or strangers for that matter). Yet in many ways, Annie is shy: her fear of not "upsetting" anyone causes much of her shyness. Annie is creative and loves journaling and scrapbooking. She has a real eye for color; having everything match is very important to her. Annie often has trouble making decisions. She fears whatever decisions she makes will hurt someone's feelings. In reality, she shows very few traits from any of her modifiers.

MEET ANNIE

Annie is 5 feet, 4 inches tall and a receptionist. She is 21 years old and single and just starting out on her own. She is the nicest person you will ever want to meet. In fact, some of her friends tell her she acts too "subservient" at times. Annie works hard to make sure everyone else is happy. She never forgets a birthday or anniversary and always sends just the right card. Annie is very intuitive about how people are feeling. Now that she is on her own and making some money, she is hoping to finally realize her dream of owning her own horse.

As a little girl, Annie had a pony and loved riding. She always felt her pony was perfect. It was very important to Annie that she and her pony both be happy. Even just thinking of her pony made her happy. As soon as she was financially able, Annie had plans to once again own an equine partner.

She wanted a horse to love, groom and perform in local area shows, and one that will meet her at the paddock gate and be ready and willing to go anywhere with her.

HORSE SEARCH

Annie has spoken with every horse owner she knows to get their opinion on what sort of horse would be a perfect match for her. She is really confused now because, of course, she doesn't want to make any of her friends unhappy by not taking their advice.

Her decisions always take a while so she isn't in any big hurry to get a horse right away. She wants her barn and stall to be perfect for her new companion before she brings him home anyway, so waiting isn't a problem at all. In fact, she is already looking for the tack she wants to use with her horse even though she doesn't yet know his size. (Note: many riders make this mistake. Unaware how important it is that the saddle and bridle fit a horse correctly, they often believe any tack fits any horse. This is why so many horses have back problems and have developed behavioral issues. See more about this on p. 168.)

What is important to her is for the horse to love her as much as she loves the horse. She needs a horse willing to stand for long periods of time allowing her to groom, braid, and "decorate" him in matching tack.

She wants a horse to be able to do many different things. He needs to do it willingly because Annie will not be forceful. She will be quiet and undemanding. You might see Annie next to her horse while she reads a book for hours.

The problem started when Annie decided, as many *Mediators* do, that the best thing she could do was to get a "rescue" horse. After all, who could better care for an "underdog" than someone who is "the nicest person you would ever want to meet"? Annie heard about a "free" horse living in the same county. The little horse was starving, standing about knee-deep in manure, and hadn't been out of his stall in a very long time. Annie was told he had been physically abused by the owners up until the time they decided there was no reason to feed him anymore. As soon as Annie heard that, she selected Lucky to be her horse. She was sure with enough love and care he would be her best friend.

THE HORSE CONNECTION

Annie quickly made arrangements to get Lucky picked up and delivered to his new home. She named him Lucky because she felt it was a stroke of luck she found him when she did. She believed that once Lucky was fattened up a little, she would be able to ride him no matter what bad habits he had. Since she had ridden a pony quite a bit as a child, she saw herself as experienced enough to handle riding Lucky.

Based on what you have read so far, is this the horse you would have picked for Annie? Well here's how her purchase worked out over time.

THE HORSE

Let's see how Lucky would score on his questionnaire.

He scored 16 as an *Actor* and 3 as a *Thinker;* and 5 as a *Worker;* Extrovert is 5, Introvert 19, Right Brain 16, Left Brain 8. The *Actor* is an *RBI*, which can make him appear quiet, obedient. However looking deeper he is also intense and distrusting, which can make him unpredictable.

The *Thinker* modifier is an *LBI*. This trait makes him clever, stubborn, and sometimes defiant but still very careful with novice riders. The *Worker* modifier is an *LBE*. This trait makes him friendly, mouthy, willful, and pushy but he will gladly work all day. Unfortunately for both Annie and Lucky, the Introvert/Extrovert boundaries are often crossed when there is a history of abuse.

With rescue horses, when there's been abuse, sometimes you have to dig a little deeper. Lucky was a nine-year-old Thoroughbred. He started his career on the racetrack, but aggressive jockeys just couldn't keep Lucky focused and stop him switching leads. Lucky was shipped off to a show barn to turn him into a jumper. However, he had been raced too young, and his knees couldn't take jumping, so he was sold to a family with teenagers looking for a horse to trail ride. The teens liked to go fast and thought a former racehorse would be just perfect for them. They also happened to like four-wheelers. Not being very horse savvy, they found it great fun to chase Lucky around and around the pasture while riding on the ATV. Lucky was kicking and running for his life; the teenagers thought he was playing and enjoying the chase as much as they did.

After that terrifying experience, Lucky just gave up. He would rear up when anyone got on him to ride and he would take off running every chance he could get. The family got so frustrated, and since they considered him a "mean" horse (because of the rearing and bolting), they just stopped feeding him. Fortunately, he was picked up by a horse rescue group. At the rescue facility, as long as he wasn't being pushed, riders could get on him and walk around the pasture. He just didn't seem to care about much of anything or anyone. The rescuers believed Lucky was a little over-reactive, but thought once he had regular groceries, he would be fine. Then along came Annie.

THE OUTCOME

In the beginning, Annie would brush Lucky, which he found very comforting, and she gave him all the hay he wanted to eat. A few months later, Lucky had a full belly, a shiny coat, and a beautiful blue blanket. Life should have been good.

Unfortunately for both, Annie decided it was time to start riding him, and dreamed of their first show. Annie thought riding the path through the woods and looking at all the spring flowers sounded like a great way to start with Lucky. However, when Annie got up on the mounting block to get on Lucky, he would not stand still. He began to fidget; backing up and going forward.

Even though the jockeys were too harsh for him, they would jump on and make him do what was expected. Remember, based on his scores, Lucky is not a confident horse. This lack of direction caused him to feel unsafe. Annie wasn't that experienced and just wanted him to love her, stand quietly and trust her. She would hop on him while he was moving but she didn't feel very confident doing so.

As a child, when Annie had ridden her pony, she would let him make all the decisions about pace and just enjoyed the view while riding along. This was not the case at all with Lucky. He kept waiting for Annie to "tell" him what to do; while at the same time, Annie thought Lucky should "know" what to do.

Lucky, still waiting for directions, didn't know what to do next. So he lurched forward at a trot. Annie just let him go and thought they would just trot right off down the path and he would settle down. With no guidance, Lucky panicked and bolted off back toward the barn. Annie began screaming. Lucky's response to her screaming was to run even faster. After all, if his leader was afraid, he should be very afraid as well. When they got back to the pasture gate, it was shut. Lucky reared up and Annie fell off.

Annie couldn't figure out what had happened to her loyal loving horse. She had fed him, brushed him and brought him back to health. Annie didn't want to do anything to correct Lucky because she didn't want him to feel he was being abused again. Annie didn't realize Lucky needed someone to give him confidence, that he needed to be told what to do—at least until he rebuilt his self-confidence.

As you might have guessed, Annie soon set out to find Lucky a new home. Lucky ended up going to a home specializing in the rehabilitation of race-horses. Annie was horseless again.

COMPARING RIDER AND HORSE

Annie is a *Mediator (RBI)* who chose Lucky, an *Actor (RBI)*. Usually this would be the perfect combination; but remember, while their Introvert components matched, Annie was not an experienced rider (even though she thought she was). Not only can right-brained horses be a handful with the meek or inexperienced rider, but when you add abuse to the mix, it takes a very experienced rider to bring them around.

Because of her lack of riding ability, Annie would have had problems with Lucky's flightiness alone. Add the fact that an *Actor* needs to look to the rider for confidence and direction, there were bound to be problems from the beginning.

When people or horses undergo a significant emotional event, it changes them, sometimes forever. Because of the abuse, Lucky needed someone who could become a more balanced personality (able to function equally in all four Social Styles) when retraining him: the trainer needed to adapt her methods to meet Lucky's needs as he moved back toward his core personality.

Lucky's personality:

- Wants to stop and think through fear.
- Likes to be given the direction and pace.
- Learns in short riding sessions.
- Depends on his rider for confidence.

Annie's personality:

- Lets the horse do what he wants safely.
- Wants to ride slowly and feel secure.
- Likes to stand and look at the scenery.
- Craves a loving horse.

Is there a perfect "buddy" for Annie? Yes, of course there is. She needs to look for a *Thinker (LBI)* with only a few *Actor (RBI)* modifiers. Even though this would not be a direct match, Annie needs a calmer horse that will think things through and take care of her.

Annie heard about a good equine rehab center and arranged for it to accept Lucky in its program. Not only that, they just happened to have a mare that had completed the rehab process and she was perfect for Annie. Annie went to meet Jazzy and deliver Lucky. It was love at first sight.

THE NEW HORSE

How did Jazzy score on her questionnaire?

She scored 20 points in the *Thinker,* and 4 points in the *Actor* categories. Extrovert scored 0, Introvert 24, Left Brain 2, Right Brain 22.

This makes Jazzy a *Thinker* with just a few *Actor* modifiers. The *Thinker* an *LBI,* is clever, curious, loves standing still, enjoys treats, and is normally great with a novice rider with Annie's personality. Jazzy would show very few other traits.

Annie and Jazzy spent many a day slowly ambling across the fields: Jazzy munching grass and Annie watching butterflies. Annie loved the long rests to just enjoy the sunshine and outdoors, and so did Jazzy. Jazzy loved to be brushed and braided, and Annie enjoyed spending hours doing so. In the spring, Annie took Jazzy to the local horse show. She liked to show in the halter class, and Jazzy excelled in the trail class. Jazzy was confident and willing to take Annie out alone and safely through any obstacles they might meet. If Jazzy should encounter anything new, she would walk up to it, put her nose on it, breathe in and out a few times and walk on. She and Annie were a perfect match.

WHAT HAPPENED TO LUCKY?

Fortunately, Lucky found the perfect home at the rehab center with trainers who knew how to align their methods with his training needs. Lucky regained his self-confidence. A very experienced rider looking for a potential Western pleasure horse adopted him.

Actors excel in disciplines that require them to be focused on their handler and know exactly where their feet are at all times. Due to so much abuse, Lucky needed an experienced rider and a job that required routine to be confident.

CHAPTER 11

Second Chances for Desperate Horses: Pain Evaluation

"I don't mean to be mean. I'm just in pain."

Overall Body Check

When your horse suddenly starts to misbehave, use a process of elimination to find the root of the problem before you start a new training program. It could be something as simple as a saddle that no longer fits. Like humans, horses change shape, which may require their saddle to be replaced four to five times over their life span. Also, when you do not ride consistently throughout the year, a saddle will fit your horse differently from spring to fall.

Behavior issues can also be caused by pain in the horse's legs or feet, pain in his mouth, or problems with his back. We discuss all these factors on the pages that follow.

SADDLE

Fitting the Horse

Finding a saddle to fit your horse is not always easy. There are several reasons you need a new saddle. These include:

1 You have purchased a new horse.

2 Your horse has substantially changed shape.

3 You have changed riding discipline.

4 Your horse is experiencing pain.

5 You are experiencing pain.

6 Your horse is displaying behavioral problems he didn't have before.

Most people go to a tack store and find a saddle they like and can afford. When they like the looks and it's comfortable, they buy it and take it home without any consideration for how it fits the horse. But this isn't the right way to get a saddle: First, you need to find a saddle that fits the horse and second, make sure it fits you.

The horse needs a saddle that:

- Doesn't pinch the withers.

- Allows for freedom of movement in the shoulder.

- Isn't too long for his back, which can cause problems in the lumbar area.

- Doesn't "bridge" thus putting pressure in places on the back (a similar feeling to having your sock twisted in your shoe).

- Is balanced and centered.

Here are a few problems that tip you off to the fact that your saddle may not be fitting your horse correctly:

- Difficulty collecting.

- Trouble turning in tight circles.

- White hairs are growing under the saddle area.

- Uneven sweat pattern from one side of the back to the other.

- Horse is irritable and unresponsive.

- Trouble extending.

- Horse flinches when touched.

- Horse moves away when you try to saddle him.

- Head bobbing that is not in sync with the horse's action or gait.

Here are several points for checking the saddle fit.

- *Withers clearance:* two fingers rule. And the gullet of the saddle should lie behind the scapula. A saddle placed too far forward will interfere with the freedom of movement of the shoulder.

- *Saddle too wide:* it should not actually sit on top of the withers, thus causing a pressure pain.

- *Saddle too narrow:* it should not pinch the sides of the withers where it can cause a pinched nerve.

- *Saddle balanced correctly over horse's center of gravity.* The deepest point should be the middle of the seat (see sidebar, p. 170).

- *Clearance of spine.* There should be no pressure directly on the spine at any point.

- *Does it "bridge"?* You can check this by putting the saddle on your horse without a pad or girth. Lay your hand flat under the front of your saddle tree and run it down the side of the tree to the back of the saddle. If you feel more space in the middle of the tree then you do at the front or back, your saddle is bridging. This can make your horse very sore backed.

- With an English saddle you should be able to see daylight from front to back along the saddle's gullet.

How to Check a Saddle's Fit

Have your horse stand square *without* a saddle.

1 Use a small round object such as a ChapStick tube, place it close to the withers and allow it to slowly roll down your horse's spine until it stops. Do this a couple times to be sure it stops at the same place on the back. This is the area of your horse's center of gravity and where he can best support your weight.

2 Apply a few pieces of duct tape from this spot straight down the side of your horse to about the midpoint of his belly on both sides.

3 Set the saddle without a pad. Be sure you first place it a bit forward on the withers and slide it back until it naturally wants to stop.

4 Take your small round object, place it at the front of the saddle and allow it to slowly roll to a stop in the seat. Look at the object's position compared to the duct tape on your horse. They should be aligned. When they are more than an inch off, the saddle does not fit well.

- With a Western saddle you should see an equal sweat pattern on both sides of the spine.

- *Girth or cinch:* when tightened, the girth should rest at least four fingers behind the horse's elbow. If not, use a shaped girth to help maintain elbow clearance.

- *Even fit:* place the saddle on the horse's back without a saddle pad approximately 2 inches behind the scapula. Stand the horse squarely and step back to observe if the saddle is sitting evenly. Neither pommel nor cantle should look higher than the other.

- *Is it too long?* A saddle that goes past the last rib may cause lumbar pain.

- *Does it gouge or rub the flank area?* The skirt of your Western saddle may do this when it is too long. (In some cases, the saddle can be taken to a leather shop and the skirt "rounded" to reduce its length.)

Fitting the Rider

Before moving on to other areas of pain for horses, let's spend just a minute on your comfort. Remember you spend as many hours "in" the saddle as your horse spends "under" it. Once you find a good fit for your horse, make sure it fits you correctly, too.

Symptoms of a saddle that does not fit you are:

- Sore ankles.

- Sore knees.

- Being unable to balance while posting.

- Hitting the back of the saddle (cantle) when cantering.

- Feeling insecure, wanting to arch your back.

Western Saddle Measurements

Rider's Weight (lbs)	5'-5' ½"	5' 1/2'- 5'9"	5'10" +
100-125	15"	16"	16"
126-185	16"	16"	16 -17"
166-250	17"-18"	17"	17"
250 +	18"	18"	18"

11.1

Western Saddles

Western saddles are measured by stirrup length and a standard seat size (fig. 11.1). The larger the seat size, the longer the stirrup.

There are many different styles of Western saddles. One saddle may work for one discipline but not for another. Once you find the saddle that fits your horse and works for your discipline put it on a saddle rack and see how it feels. Is it comfortable?

1 Do your legs hang correctly? With your legs hanging down out of the stirrups, look at placement. If your legs are too far forward of the stirrup, the seat is too small. If your legs hang behind the stirrups it may be too large.

2 Do you have at least an inch of clearance between your thigh and the pommel (front of the saddle)?

3 Can you put a three finger-widths between your bottom and the cantle (back of saddle)?

Stirrup fender placement is the key in Western saddles. When you sit in the saddle and let your legs hang free, they should lie over the natural curve in the fender. When they are in front or behind the fender, the saddle does not fit you correctly.

English Saddles

There are a few areas you can easily check for fit on your English saddle:

1 Can you put a hand-width between your crotch and the pommel?

English Saddle Measurements

Buttock-to-Knee Measurement	Saddle Size
Up to 16"	15"
From 16 ½"-18 ½"	16"
From 18 ½"-20"	16 1/2"-17"
Up to 21 ½"	17"
Up to 23"	17 ½"
Up to 23 ½"	18"

11.2

2 Do you have 3 or 4 inches between your buttocks and the back of the saddle?

3 Does your leg hang down comfortably? Can you run an imaginary string from your ear down through your shoulder to the back of your heel?

One other important saddle measurement is the "twist," which is the narrowest part toward the front of the saddle. The type of twist you need depends on your pelvis and your inner thigh muscles. In general, a man has a flatter thigh and will need a wider twist; a woman has a rounder thigh so will need a narrower twist.

If your saddle is too large for you it will be hard to maintain a correct seat position. It will be a constant battle to avoid riding in a "chair-seat" position. Your posting will not be small and smooth as it should be, but rather a huge effort at popping up and down.

If your saddle is too small for you it will cause you to hit the cantle while cantering and make you tip forward while posting.

When seated correctly (with the exception of the saddle for saddle-seat riding), there should be an imaginary vertical line dropping down from your shoulder, through your hip to your heel.

To measure yourself for your saddle, sit on a straight chair with your back against the chair's back with your feet flat on the floor in front of you. Your hip and thigh should form a right angle, as should the bend of your knee. On one side, measure from the back of your buttocks to the back of your knee. Enlist a friend to help if needed. This is your buttock-to-knee measurement (fig. 11.2).

It is always a good idea to find a good professional saddle fitter for help in this matter of such importance.

> **Note** We highly recommend two books and two DVDS on saddle fitting by Dr. Joyce Harman, DVM, MRCVS: *The Horse's Pain-Free Back and Saddle-Fit Book; The Western Horse's Pain-Free Back and Saddle-Fit Book; English Saddles: How to Fit Pain-Free* (DVD); *Western Saddles: How to Fit Pain-Free* (DVD). All are available from Trafalgar Square Books (www.horseandriderbooks.com).

LEGS AND FEET

The horse's feet and legs are the next place to check for pain. The old saying "No foot, No horse" is truer than you might think. Look at your horse's stance. While he is standing in a relaxed position, does he stand squarely on all four feet? Does he look like he is standing underneath himself too much? This could be a sign of back pain. Does he look like he is "camped" out (back feet out behind, not vertical)? This can be his conformation, or a sign of pain.

Is the horse leaning to his back feet? Trying to take pressure off the front legs is always a sign of pain; it could be navicular or founder problems. While observing your horse while on flat ground, notice whether he always has one leg in front of the other whenever he stops. This could be a back leg or a front leg, but it might be a sign that he is uncomfortable or in pain. If a horse is physically sound and standing on flat ground, he will stand square on all four feet.

Symptoms of pain in legs or feet can be:

- Lameness.
- Cracks in hoof wall.
- Seedy toe or white line disease.
- Foul odor (thrush).
- Tendon strains.
- Body soreness.
- Toe lands first.
- Standing with legs too far under the body.
- Standing with back legs too far out behind.
- Stumbling.
- Toeing out with front feet.
- Not wanting to move.
- Not wanting to stand still.
- Head-bobbing while moving (out of sync with action or gait).
- Head-tossing.

As you can see, there are many things to consider. His behavior may just be due to his conformation or his personality, but it may also be a problem related to pain.

TEETH

A full dental work-up by an equine dentist is another recommendation. Dental problems may not only cause weight loss but also affect the horse's gait, temperament, and flexibility. If you don't believe it, put your head all the way back, clamp your teeth really tightly together and lower your chin to your chest. Did your teeth slide? Of course they did. Now take a horse with teeth problems that don't allow the teeth to "slide" properly and ask him to collect and tuck his chin. And when the bit is hitting wolf teeth on a young horse, you might find yourself on a horse that is standing on his back feet only when you pull back on the reins!

Some indicators of teeth problems include:

- Abnormal change in behavior or dropping feed while eating, excessive salivation, head tilt.

- Sipping water intermittently while eating hay or grain.

- Quidding (dropping "balls" of hay from mouth).

- Large particles of hay or grain in manure.

- Poor topline ("sway back").

- Too high or too low head carriage.

- Unwillingness to move forward or backward.

- Lameness.

- Packing food in cheeks.

- Large forehead muscles, or one side larger than the other.

- Incisors not centered (the top and bottom teeth do not match up).

- Bad mouth odor.

- Slow eater.

- Won't accept a bit (excessive chewing, head-tossing, fidgeting).

- Head-shaking.

- Difficulty with flexion.

- Trouble taking leads.

- Loss of weight/condition.

- Turning head to side when chewing.

- Raising head up high when chewing.

- Choke (condition caused by missing teeth or sharp ridges).

Some visuals that could indicate teeth problems include:

- Stance: horse doesn't stand "square" (one or more feet is extended).

- Hollow back.

- Ewe neck.

- Hollow flanks.

- Dip in hindquarters.

- Uneven eyes and/or nostrils.

When you have a vet or equine dentist, be sure to ask him to check:

- Points.

- Waves.

- Parroting.

- Hooks.

- Overbite.

- Underbite.

- Missing or misaligned teeth.

- Wolf teeth.

Horses can also have loose teeth. Young horses, under six years, can retain caps that will need to be removed. Horses can also fracture a tooth by picking up something hard in their food. In fact, some horses with tooth pain will pick up pebbles to chew; it seems to relieve the pain but can fracture a tooth. A horse may also try to relieve toothache by dunking his head repeatedly into the water tank (not in a playful way). Take the horse's temperature, and if it is too high, contact an equine dentist or vet immediately.

Remember, these are just indicators and the horse may or may not have a problem with his teeth. However, when you have more than one of these signs, it is a good idea to contact a professional for an evaluation.

BACK

If the teeth are all fine, check the horse's back. A good equine chiropractor can quickly determine if your horse has something out of place. Imagine your back goes out—you can barely force yourself to stand up straight—then a friend jumps on your back and expects you to carry her around the room.

We do that to our horses all the time. They are stoic and mostly just take it, but once in a while, it just gets to be too much, and their behavior changes. Tragically, the old saying, "The floggings will continue until the attitude improves," is the motto of some owners. So before you try any corrective training, make sure the skeletal structure of your horse is sound.

Ask your equine chiropractor to teach you how to monitor your horse's back for "bumps" that shouldn't be there. And, if your saddle doesn't fit properly, chances are your horse's back will repeatedly need the same chiropractic treatment. Many times, when the rider has a back problem, eventually her horse will have a back problem in exactly the same area. At a recent clinic, an equine chiropractor brought out 12 people and examined their backs; he then brought out their 12 horses and matched every horse to every rider perfectly. Getting your horse's back fixed might even help your back in the long run.

SOFT-TISSUE ISSUES

Finally, a good massage for a hard-working horse is always welcomed. Someone who does massage and provides chiropractic care is a good find! A chiropractor can find skeletal problems while a massage therapist can find soft-tissue problems. Sometimes both the skeleton and the soft tissue need to be examined to find the underlying problem. Your massage therapist can show you simple massage techniques that take very little time. With just a few minutes a day, a massage can help the muscle tone around the horse's back and shoulder area.

When you have eliminated any physical problems your horse might be experiencing, it is time to look at training options.

PART FOUR

Training Techniques for Your Horse's Social Style

CHAPTER 12

Training: What to Expect

Creating the Balanced Horse

The last section of this book is designed to help you understand training by taking the personality of each horse into account. Building a relationship with a horse is no different than building any other team partnership. In order to have a more *balanced* horse, you must identify all his traits and work to eliminate the negative ones and replace them with positive ones.

When you want to train a *new* horse it is critical you take the time to do it right. We know it can be frustrating and time-consuming. But by now you must understand that all people do not fit all horses (and vice versa), and that some horse personalities are better than others at various disciplines.

According to studies on human team building, as a newly formed team, you go through four stages: "*storming,*" "*norming,*" *conforming*, and finally, *performing*. The first few times the team meets, there is no trust between its members. They will be very guarded in what they say and will keep conversations superficial. Later meetings will find people starting to normalize and trust each other more. Still later, the team will start to conform to each other and ideas will be shared. Finally, the group will start performing as a "team" with common goals and trust.

Your new horse partner will have a similar view of life. When you first meet, most horses won't fully trust you. Over time, they will form an opinion about the type of relationship they are willing to have with you.

Most of this will be based on aligning Social Styles. As time passes, the horse and rider will conform to each other's personal traits. Finally, you will perform as a team with trust and a bond. Have you ever heard people say, "All I have to do is think about what I want to do next and my horse does it?" That's when you know you have reached the "performing" stage and are totally in tune with your horse.

WHAT BEHAVIORS CAN YOU LIVE WITH?

One of the first things you want to determine is what you can live with should everything go very wrong. A horse's basic response to stress may be the deal breaker: for example, if you cannot ride a horse that bucks, a *Thinker* is probably not an option for you (fig. 12.1).

Thinker—At play, you might see him just standing and enjoying playing "face tag" with the other horses, but with his human partner, he can become pushy during groundwork. And when upset or stressed being ridden, he has a tendency to buck.

Worker—This horse may remind you of a boisterous child. When being led, he can become disrespectful to the handler, and when being ridden, he can bite you or another horse, and strike out when upset or stressed.

Actor—This horse can be unpredictable. He can be shy, or he can seem to want to be "in your pocket." His reaction to stress can be to kick without warning. He can freeze, then suddenly bolt. He can also go so "inward" that he will *appear* calm when he is anything but.

Talker—This horse has a tendency to rear. At play, you might see him rearing more than you do other horses in the herd. With his human partner, rearing may become his way of communication. When stressed, he may bolt.

Common Stress Responses

Thinker	Worker	Actor	Talker
Bucks; pushes into handler	Bites; strikes	Kicks behind; shuts down mentally	Bolts; rears

12.1

Having been involved with horses for most of our lives, we have seen many different problems associated with training, owning, showing, and trail riding horses. Our desire with this training section is to help everyone be a better trainer. Every minute you spend with your horse is a training situation. While you may not view it as such, the horse most certainly will. The horse is constantly taking in his environment. Remember, the horse is a prey animal; survival depends on his reading everything—all the time. You may not even notice the constant testing for herd position. Even your most subtle body language can make a difference in your relationship with your horse.

While this is written with someone who wants to train her horse in mind, we believe everyone can benefit from the information being shared because as just said, every time you ride you are, in effect, training your horse. As a trainer of many different horses, you will eventually encounter every horse personality. Knowing how to read and align to each horse's personality is critical. When you train you want to consider the experience levels of both you and your horse.

Perhaps you just want to train and enjoy the horse you now own. Answering the questionnaires we have provided for you and your horse will be invaluable (pp. 21 and 78). If you find you do not align with the horse you currently own, there is no shame in admitting it's a personality conflict.

Allow yourself and your horse to find the perfect partner. And when your personalities do not align, but you don't want to sell your horse, don't fret: our research shows that after a while, people who took the time to communicate appropriately found most horses could align to their personality. What you need to understand is this might take weeks, months, or even years.

Each person is different in how long she chooses to try and make it work, though in some cases, it may never happen. When you own a horse that you have no desire to work with, or really care about, it's time to think about what this does to you and the horse. Is it fair to not enjoy each other?

There are occasions when you cannot get rid of a horse and being honest, most horses don't care whether they are ridden or not. That said, all horses need to be cared for and to be a part of the herd. That could be with other horses, another animal such as a goat, or with their "human" herd. If you provide the basics, the horse will be alright. But, will that be enough for you? If this is the only horse you own, will you be enjoying your dream of horse ownership? A horse is a lifetime commitment, to him, to you. Our hope is that commitment is a happy one.

So whether you are an owner, trainer, buyer or seller, we want this book to help you have a more successful experience.

On trails you will likely be riding with a group of horses with a variety of personalities. Remember horses learn in different ways. If you encounter

What if You Have the Wrong Horse?

As we have shown, there is a horse personality to match each human personality. When both personalities match, it will provide more enjoyment for all. But what if you are feeling uncomfortable with your horse? You might feel you are just not bonding.

This is when you have to make a decision. You may decide to keep this horse because you love him, can't afford another one, don't want to face the search process, or feel you can eventually learn to get along with him. If the latter, you may have to find a qualified trainer to work with. When you love the horse enough, it may be worth working on the relationship. You may need to change your personality to better fit your horse. In some cases, over an extended period of time a horse will pick up enough traits from the horse Social Style that matches his rider's.

Just remember, not every horse can change easily. It may be a long process, and he will always revert back to his core Social Style under extreme stress. The extroverted horse will always want to move and not like standing still, while the introverted horse will always need to rest more and not like moving forward for long periods of time.

As people grow older, their personality often changes to some degree and the hope is they achieve a more balanced style. Horses may also balance their personality as they grow older. They just require a little patience, love, and understanding.

What if you can only afford one horse and the one you have isn't a match? It is perfectly okay to sell such a horse: remember, your worst nightmare could be someone else's dream horse. Also, consider the possibility your horse may be happier with another owner who has a matching personality.

If you decide to search for another horse, it can be very helpful to work with an instructor, trainer, or breeder. Don't consider it a failure when the horse you purchased isn't a perfect match.

Sometimes a person will buy a horse and fall in love with him, only to find he doesn't enjoy doing the things she likes to do. If that happens and you can afford another horse, pick one that does enjoy your discipline or activities.

something on the trail that frightens the horses, some will need to stop their feet and deal with it, while others will need to keep their feet moving.

Unless there has been discussion beforehand, group trail riding may not be a good place to train your horse. If your horse is inexperienced, be sure to know your horse, know yourself and how you plan to deal with scary situations well in advance of the ride. Then, to be safe, pick people to accompany you who understand, and can possibly help you deal with your horse should the occasion arise.

Horse Component Comparisons: Training in a Nutshell

The Introvert:
- Learns to sidepass easier from a stand still.

The Extrovert:
- Learns to sidepass easier when taught on the move.

Left-Brained:
- Enjoys being "off line" or at liberty.
- Learns better when each training session offers something different.
- Gets bored easily.
- Likes to go new places.

Right-Brained:
- Finds it difficult being "off line" or at liberty.
- Finds comfort in doing circles or repetition.
- Does better with shorter training sessions.
- Needs something to focus on to relax, such as riding around cones.

INTRODUCING YOURSELF

When you are bringing a new horse home you need to understand that horses live by instinct. They "read" a human's intentions and act accordingly. Since you want your new horse to understand that you really do care about his welfare, it is wise to take some time getting to know each other. It is human nature to have a tendency to rush things like this. Just slowing down to give the horse time to find comfort in your presence go a long way toward a successful relationship. It also gives you time to understand his personality.

One of the first things I like to do with a new horse is sit on a bucket or bale of hay in front of the stall. I can watch him, and it allows him to observe me without pressure. I may even read a magazine and just let him know I will be there for him. I use this time to see how he is settling in and if he is

Groundwork: Problems and Solutions

THINKER	WORKER	ACTOR	TALKER
Will lag behind when leading. (Make rapid turns in opposite directions, he will pick up the pace and stay with you.)	Will try to lead you instead of walking with you. (Learn to back him up by wiggling lead line; when he gets in front, wiggle until he backs up.)	Usually leads well but spooks into you. (Stay alert and focused on where you are going so he has confidence in you.)	Will walk all over you. (Keep him focused and keep him at your speed, not his.)
Pushy, standing in your space. (Use large body language and back him up away from you, release and give reward.)	Pushy, rubbing on you with disrespect. (Use "big" body language; shake the rope so he has to back up.)	Faces you on longe line. (Beforehand be sure he goes out to the circle and comes back quietly and easily, then start longeing slowly.)	Stops on the longe; quickly switches direction. (Snake the line and ask him to stop. Interrupt the pattern and reward.)
Slow to drop his head. (Wait him out; keep steady pressure and reward for slightest try.)	Drops his head then walks off. (Wiggle the lead so he has to back up then ask for the head drop again.)	Drops head then goes backward. (Use soft words, rub and comfort; repeat the task.)	Drops head then takes off in any direction. (Ask for small "tries" and as he complies, allow him to raise his head; then you walk off deciding on the direction.)
Doesn't want to move his feet. (Turn and walk, then stop and reward. He will enjoy pleasing you when rewarded.)	Doesn't want to stand still. (Don't force him but when he stops, reward and ask him to move his feet around a circle. Then ask him to stand again.)	Is afraid to move. (Ask him to drop his head and relax; rub then walk off in large circle until calm; reward.)	Is afraid to stand still. (Walk in large circle; make it smaller as he slows down and stops; then walk until calm and will stand.)

12.2

relaxed or curious about me and his new surroundings. When he is, he has more left-brained tendencies. When he is pacing, pinning his ears, or whinnying for other horses, he has right-brained tendencies. All these will give you a window into your horse's personality and clues as to how and when to start the training process.

When it comes to horses, less is always more. If a horse can feel a fly land on his mane, he can also feel your hand at the end of the lead rope or longe line. Keep your hands light on the rein or lead, thus allowing the horse to feel when you squeeze and wait for your next request.

PROBLEM AREAS

Here are difficulties to be aware of when training the different Social Styles. Interestingly enough, these areas are what make one horse better at a certain riding discipline than another.

Every individual method of teaching horses a specific task is based on doing it the same way for all of them. But, you should be aware that different horse personalities learn or understand differently. Take a look at the charts containing groundwork and riding problems (and solutions) that may help you better understand the four core horse personalities (figs. 12.2 and 12.3).

Now we'll take an in-depth look at each horse personality—*Thinker, Worker, Actor, Talker*—from the training perspective.

Riding Problems and Solutions

THINKER	WORKER	ACTOR	TALKER
Doesn't want to move. (Kicking makes him dull; instead, turn his head and disengage his hind end to get him going.)	Won't stand still. (Ride in circles; make each one smaller until you disengage hind end and he stops. Don't make him stand too long.)	Afraid to move. (Rub, talk softly, use minimum aids and move off in a circle until he is calm.)	Afraid to stand still. (Don't make him stop; ride in circles out to bigger ones and into smaller ones until he can focus and stop his feet.)
Lazy. (He is bored; go somewhere else and keep him busy.)	Naughty. (He is bored; he needs to go somewhere else and with speed.)	Always alert. (He finds comfort in being in the same place; do short sessions in new areas.)	Unfocused. (He needs repetition so he can focus on the work.)
Likes music and riding freestyle.	Has an active mind; likes long rides, and jumping.	Likes to be told what to do; enjoys dressage and arena work.	Wants to go fast; enjoys racing and contesting/gymkhana events.
Wants to go too slowly. (Ask him to go even slower; then he will "want" to go faster.)	Wants to go too fast. (Make small circles; when he slows go larger; when he speeds up, go smaller.)	Lateral work/side-passing. (He learns better one small step at a time. Teach from a standstill.)	Lateral work/sidepassing. (He learns better while moving.)
Happiest when out of the arena—not making circles.	Happiest when going at a faster pace and getting change of scenery.	Happiest when he can go slowly and stay in same environment.	Happiest when he can go faster and work in repetitions.

12.3

CHAPTER 13

The Thinker (LBI)

Inventive, Food-Oriented, Curious

The **Thinker** is a horse that can be quick and do things in short bursts. Think of a sprinter. He is usually calm and can be bold when required. He needs to think things through. Take your time. He may not appear to be the fastest horse but trust us, he can move. He just has to be motivated (fig. 13.1).

> **Caution**
>
> When feeling playful, this horse may buck.

WHICH DISCIPLINE AND WHY

The **Thinker** is usually good at:

- *Roping*—Quick to run out behind the cow; thinks about what the cow is doing, will stop and hold, then is happy to go back to the rail and stand quietly while waiting for the next cow.

- *Therapy work*—Normally very calm, doesn't get upset with an unbalanced rider. Walks very slowly and stands for a long time. Loves to be groomed.

- *Driving*—Is calm, thinks about traffic and "desensitizes" quickly.

- *Competitive trail*—Will lower his head, look at an obstacle and then confidently move through. Also likes the variety and doesn't get rattled about new challenges.

- *Trail (shorter rides)*—Likes the trail, finds it interesting, and stays calm. He is not an endurance horse; gets tired mentally after two hours, or less.

- *Racing (quarter mile)*—Can start quickly but will not run long distances.

*Note: See chapter 8, p. 121, for more on riding disciplines and activities for the **Thinker**.*

Thinker: Character Strengths & Weaknesses

STRENGTHS	WEAKNESSES
• Persistent	• Non-responsive
• Loyal	• Lazy
• Thoughtful	• Pushy
• Well behaved	• Stubborn
• Loves being groomed	• Defiant
• Food-oriented	• Unforgiving

13.1

THINKER TRAITS TO CONSIDER

- When being longed, he will stop easily but not come in to you unless he feels there's a reason. Extra rubs or scratches when he does well will get better results.

- Being longed, he may be "slow" to leave you and go out on the circle. We have seen people who are training their horse get frustrated and say, "He just won't go out." This horse doesn't see a need for longeing.

- Doing repetitive work is the worst thing for this personality. He has problems moving fluidly. His boredom will show up by his becoming dull or unresponsive.

TRAINING TIPS AND TECHNIQUES

- Give this horse a purpose. Without one he will become dull.

- Ask slowly, take your time. He needs to think things out.

- Give incentives: a good rest, a scratch, maybe a treat.

- Don't let him become the leader. When he wants to go slowly, don't force him to go fast; instead, slow him down even more.

- When this horse wants to go too fast, ask him to go even faster. He will then willingly slow down.

- Don't use too much repetition. Once this horse knows his job, he can become defiant when asked to repeat it.

- Don't be fooled into thinking he is lazy. He is usually very clever at making you think he is lazy!

- Don't allow him to intimidate you. Be firm but not overly aggressive.

- Wait until he chooses to work with you. If you run up to him and toss on the halter, he will stand there as if all is well, until you turn to walk away. Most likely he will still be just standing there. Take a little more time with him. We always suggest "meeting and greeting" any horse, but for the *Thinker*, this is a big deal. He wants a good scratch and likes to think about the day ahead.

- If you have greeted him and he doesn't follow you, you must now think like a leader. Use "larger" body language; be very clear on what you are asking. If he still won't move, try to lead him in the opposite direction. This puts him off balance and he will have to move his feet. Once the feet are moving, reward him and he should be fine.

- If something spooks or worries this horse, don't try to rush him past it. Come up to it slowly, let him stop and think. Give a rub and tell him it is okay. Walk up a few more steps and stop again. Once he changes from worry to curiosity, he will put his nose on it, or drop his head and look for something to eat. Then you can move right on by every time.

- Making the *Thinker* go in circles is torture for him (the reason why he doesn't like being longed. He works much better when "going somewhere." When in an arena, put cones in various places. Instead of riding along the rail over and over, try going from cone to cone; going to the rail and around the arena a few times; then back to the cones. Be sure to give this horse plenty of rest between tasks. Train for 20 minutes in the ring working on speed, for instance, then go outside it and do some lateral work down the fence for a while. Finally, go out to the trail to work on backing up.

- The *Thinker* works hard to "outthink" his rider at times. The best way to work with this is to do more of what the horse wants: for instance, if you want to move along with some energy and he slows down, try telling him that going slow is a good idea, but make him go even slower. He will soon think he wants to speed up. If you start the day and he wants to canter when you would rather trot, trust me, let him canter and soon enough, he will want to trot. The *Thinker* horse likes to believe he has some say in what the day will bring.

Remember both the *Thinker* and the *Worker* become bored easily, and when the *Thinker* becomes bored, he becomes dull or lazy. The *Thinker* also does not have the endurance of the *Worker*.

PERSONALITY PITFALLS WITH THE *THINKER*

Human Introverts
Analyst—The *Thinker* is your best match; however, you need to watch that your desire for perfection doesn't bore the horse to the point of frustration.

Mediator—You understand the need to take it slowly, allowing this horse to dwell on the task. However, you must guard against the horse pushing you around and taking advantage of you.

Human Extroverts
Powerful—The *Thinker* will work hard for you, but only for short bursts. You need to learn to show him when you are pleased, rewarding him with "rubs" and giving him breaks.

Advocate—You will need to work hard to get along with the *Thinker*. Slow down; let him have time to think before doing what you ask. If you push too hard, he might try to buck you off.

*Note: The aggressive rider might cause the **Thinker** to become frustrated, which results in bad behavior such as bucking, or locking up and not wanting to move.*

PUTTING IT IN PRACTICE

Marry's Case Study: *Traveler*

Let's look at a **Thinker** mismatched with a **Powerful** who did not align with her horse.

When Judy, an intermediate rider, called me to get help, her Morgan horse, Traveler had put her in the hospital for the second time. Judy told me she had been able to ride Traveler bareback with a halter and lead rope when she first got him and had not experienced any problems. She was happy with Traveler for the first few months. Over time, however, he became dangerous. When she was on the ground, he would bite, push her out of the way to get through the barn door; he had even tried to charge and attack her.

When I first met Traveler I did a quick visual assessment and determined the following indications of a **Thinker**:

- Eyes large and wide-set on his forehead: left-brained.

- Large round jowl: usually left-brained.

- Wide-set ears: left-brained.

- Would pin his ears, but watched quietly: Introvert.

During this first meeting I also looked at Traveler for pain issues. He was 10 years old and stood 15.2 hands. His back was long for a Morgan and his throatlatch was fairly thick. This told me he was not going to be able to collect easily. By the look of his calm eyes, he appeared relaxed and not in any pain.

He carried his head normally, not too high or too low, and did not appear worried or nervous. I did find he had a pinched nerve in the withers and his feet needed trimming, both of which we got fixed.

Once these physical problems were dealt with, Traveler:

- Was calm until his owner was present, then he would have a concerned and angry look in his eye. However, he did not become aggressive toward me.

- Flexed easily.

- Lowered his head without worry.

- Backed up (after some work).

- Was not compelled to move his feet until I asked.

All of this was more evidence to me that Traveler's core personality was a *Thinker*.

On my next visit, Judy picked up a rope halter with a lead and stepped into Traveler's corral. He took off to the other side. Every time she stepped toward him, he pinned his ears and ran 20 more feet, then stopped. From this reaction, I gathered he was clever, defiant, and didn't want to move his feet any more than necessary. (More proof he was a *Thinker*.) Judy ran him into a large stall and was able to halter him. With his ears pinned and his eyes almost pinched closed, I could tell this horse did not like Judy at all!

On my first training session, I became the Introvert and worked with him on leading. He led easily, and was quiet. Knowing that a *Thinker* does not like arena work, I set up cones and a tarp. He was not spooked at the new obstacles and walked across the tarp without concern.

Next I wanted to see how he would do at longeing. I asked him to back out of my space, and then move off to the right. This is where the trouble started.

He pinned his ears, lunged forward, stopped and turned to go the other way. When I bumped the rope, he came charging straight for me. I managed to move out of the way, became an Extrovert and bumped the rope hard to make him back up. He did stop and back up, then stood glaring at me but did not move his feet. I returned to being an Introvert and just stood and watched him transform mentally again as I didn't ask him to move. He went back to the quiet horse I had started with earlier. I had seen both fight and fear in that short time.

I started again, asking him very slowly to perform various movements. For each movement he did correctly, I gave him a verbal reward and let him stand. So it went like this: "Back," stop and stand for a few seconds. Then, "Move the shoulder over" and stand. Then, "Walk forward." By breaking down each movement into a task and not a demand, he began to try. His head was still higher than I would have liked and his ears were still pinned but he did not threaten to run me down again.

A conversation with Judy revealed what had happened. Judy was a *Powerful*, used to being in control. She had heard longeing was good for a horse, so longeing she did: she would continuously longe him for 40 minutes or more. She would ask him to trot or canter the whole time with no rest. This was the beginning of the end for Traveler. Extended longeing without a break is bad for any horse, but for a *Thinker* it is torture. He soon learned to hate Judy. She had pushed him too far and he found the only way to get relief was to fight, so he would charge at her. Only then could he stop moving.

I worked with this horse for two more weeks. I was always aware of my body language, asking slowly, and giving a reward for small tries. I did not ask him to work out of his comfort zone. I gave him jobs that were more about change of direction and transitions, and less about routine.

Once the groundwork was going well, I decided it was time to ride. We found Judy's saddle did not fit correctly and that was causing an issue with his withers. Once he had a well-fitting saddle, I was pleasantly surprised at how well he did under tack. In the beginning he struggled with standing still at the mounting block. I think part of this was from Judy not realizing she was stabbing the toe of her boot into his side every time she got on. Once he realized that was not going to happen, and the saddle fit properly, he stood quietly.

While riding, Traveler was very receptive to words of praise. I used reverse psychology on him for speed. If he was walking out slowly, I would tell him "Good boy," and ask him to move even slower. He then happily went at a nice walk when I asked for it. If his trot was too fast, I would ask him to speed it up and it didn't take long before he was happy to trot very slowly. After a couple weeks of riding, I turned him back over to Judy.

I went through all the changes and how to have a happy willing horse with Judy. Unfortunately, Judy couldn't, or wouldn't, change her personality to fit Traveler's. A few months later Judy called to tell me Traveler had put her in the Emergency Room again. He had gotten so mad and tired of the pressure she put on him that he bit the top of her head requiring quite a few stitches. I told her then, for her safety and his happiness, to find him a new home. She replied that she was too attached and, "By golly, they would work through this."

A year later, I received a letter that Traveler had been sold. A man, an *Analyst,* I had spoken to before who knew the problems Judy had with him was willing to try him out. With their matching personalities, Traveler became a well-respected Mounted Police horse.

CHAPTER 14

The Worker (LBE)

Friendly, Willful, Hard-Working

The *Worker*, as his name implies, works: "Give me a job and let me go at it." This horse does not like standing around, looking at the scenery; he likes to go.

The *Worker* is ready to jump in the trailer for the next adventure. Not much worries him and he sees no need to stand and think about it.

This horse can be friendly but willful and is not always respectful of your space. This is a confident horse with a lot of endurance. He enjoys moving and has high energy (fig. 14.1).

Caution

In extreme fear or playfulness, this horse might bite or strike.

WHICH DISCIPLINE AND WHY

The *Worker* is usually good at:

- *Cutting*—Is athletic and bold, likes to do his job.

- *Eventing*—Has the endurance and confidence needed for this discipline and has the heart to jump round the cross-country course.

- *Liberty*—Excels off line.

- *Tricks*—Likes to play.

- *Trail riding*—The *Worker* is one of the personalities best suited for an all-day trail ride. He thrives on going forward, seeing new places and new things.

*Note: See chapter 8, p. 121, for more disciplines and activities for the **Worker**.*

Worker: Character Strengths & Weaknesses

STRENGTHS	WEAKNESSES
• Playful	• Naughty
• Friendly	• Willful
• Adventurous	• "Mouthy"
• Competitive	• Resistant
• Confident	• Impatient
• Independent	• Argumentative
• Leads	• Stubborn

14.1

WORKER TRAITS TO CONSIDER

- He doesn't understand the need for moving laterally.

- He feels backing up is not necessary.

- He views standing still as boring because he has a need to move.

- He considers being on a longe line as restrictive. He likes moving forward and out. This horse may test your strength trying to hold him back.

TRAINING TIPS AND TECHNIQUES

- Be very creative. This horse gets bored easily.

- Give him some days of just play. He will appreciate it and work harder for you.

- Change the scenery. This horse is good at arena work for short sessions, but then needs to be outside or on a trail to keep his mind sharp.

- Don't punish too harshly for disobedience. He usually thinks it's a game. Be assertive, maybe a bump on the lead, or a small leg bump when riding and then just move on. If you make a big deal of it, he will too!

- Don't force the *Worker* to move too slowly.

- Don't work with him on a line that is too short. He can become bad tempered because he needs space.

- The *Worker* is usually standing at the gate waiting to be put to work. However, if you have bored him too often, he can be the hardest one to catch and will make a game of it.

- When being longed and he gets bored, he can buck or kick out. Don't stop and reprimand him, just push him up a little harder, or change direction, maybe give him a verbal sound like "sssshhh" to let him know you don't appreciate his games. Be firm but not aggressive.

- The hardest job for this horse is arena work. If you must do it, keep changing your speed, and make transitions up and down. Change direction often. Keep this type of work at a minimum. The *Worker* learns quickly.

- The *Worker* has self-confidence and likes new adventures. Take him out on the trail, vary the speed, and find a jump or two. He is the type of horse with whom you can enjoy the world.

- If you have a child who likes to go and go, this is the horse you need. He will take care of himself and, by default, the child, too.

- An important point to note for trail riders is that left-brained horses need to be trusted. When you have an experienced *Worker* who has never refused to go forward and he suddenly refuses, listen to him! Too many times, a rider has pushed a *Worker*, even though he doesn't want to go through a creek or down a steep hill, and both ended up in quicksand or in a big hole. *Workers* know what's not safe so trust them!

- Working at liberty off line is usually very productive.

When dealing with the *Worker*, understanding his personality is most important: both the *Talker* and the *Worker* are *forward-moving* horses but they have different reasons for this behavior. The *Talker* moves out of a fear-based instinct. The *Worker* moves because he is confident and "wants" to go forward. He views anything else as boring or not necessary.

PERSONALITY PITFALLS WITH THE *WORKER*

Human Extroverts

Powerful—You are the best match because you enjoy all-day rides. Be careful you pay attention to this horse's behavior. He can easily become pushy and "mouthy" when not asked to behave.

Advocate—This personality type will also work for you as long as you understand the *Worker* needs to make some decisions. If you force him to always do it your way and at the speed you want, he can go into fight mode—with resulting bad behavior.

Note: The not-so-confident rider will give this type of horse an opportunity to not listen to her and "play" or get pushy instead.

Human Introverts

Analyst—Don't ask the *Worker* to go too slowly or bore him with each step being managed by you. Let him make some decisions on speed and direction.

Mediator—You will need to work on matching the energy of this horse. If you just "go along for the ride," it may be faster than you had planned.

Note: An overconfident rider can push this horse into fighting back, which can make him "mean."

PUTTING IT IN PRACTICE

Marry's Case Study: *King*

King is an 11-year-old Quarter Horse pony, initially trained as a barrel horse and later sold as a trail horse. King loved being on the trail. He had never been worked on the ground or taught any manners. He was owned by Heidi, a *Mediator,* who lacked confidence.

When I met King, my quick visual assessment determined his:

- Conformation was correct with nothing out of balance physically: left-brained.

- Head was small with a wide forehead and large, alert eyes: left-brained.

- Ears were small and "foxy": extroverted.

- Legs set square but he had no desire to stand still: extroverted.

King's facial expression said, "I want to enjoy life." He looked friendly, as if he wanted to get to know me. Not understanding how to stay out of my space, he walked up, then tried to walk over me. He was not doing this in a mean way; he had not been taught any manners. When I rubbed his shoulder, he immediately started rubbing his nose on my arm. But since I did not correct him immediately and ignored his behavior, he became bored and began to paw at nothing. Based on all these traits, I decided King was a *Worker.*

King was a very athletic, good-looking horse with very alert eyes, ready for action. Here were some of his behavior patterns:

- He didn't have any boundaries because he hadn't been taught to respect anyone or anything. "Boundary" issues are found in the Extrovert more than any other type.

- When his owner led him around, he dragged her everywhere. He liked making all the decisions.

- When she was in the saddle, he tended to try and go in the direction he chose instead of the direction being asked. If she had been less nervous, he might have been more responsive, but he was allowed to get away with this sort of behavior. (This was an example of what happens when a less confident *Mediator* rides a *Worker* with few manners.)

- King didn't want to repeat an exercise once he had learned it. He got bored easily. When Heidi wanted to ride in the arena for an hour, he became resistant.

Heidi wanted a horse that would go anywhere—and safely. In a sense, King was that horse, but only for the right person. Heidi was nervous because King wanted to move all the time—he didn't like standing around. Even though King would have safely taken her down a road with a lot of traffic or over the roughest trail, Heidi couldn't give up wanting to be the one in control even though she did not have the necessary confidence.

As I said earlier, a *Worker* is usually safe but often is "on a mission" and doesn't feel he needs to be told how to do anything. When you start "telling" him, a battle can start.

When learning some groundwork, King liked to be in "your space." He struggled with lateral work, not liking to step his front end over. He also did not want to stand still or back up. He would have to give over control and it was not something he planned to do.

I quickly determined that I would have to be a confident and assertive (not aggressive) Extrovert with this horse.

When I first began training sessions with King, I did the following:

- To make him understand he would have to "tolerate" my requests, I asked him to stand still. When he began pawing, or became frustrated (after about 10 seconds) I would allow him to move his feet, but only in my direction. I walked him in a small circle coming back to the exact place we started. Once he realized that being impatient got him nowhere, he decided to stand longer. When he behaved and stood, I took him somewhere new.

- He complied when I asked for a "head down" but then it would pop right back up. Again, not getting frustrated, I asked again for the "head down." When he dropped it and left it down for 10 seconds, I called this a success and moved on.

- On the longe line, King did well at going out onto the circle, but he wanted to move forward at his speed only. I worked quite a bit on transitions, and I didn't keep him on the same circle: I went from one end of the arena to the other to keep him focused and able to listen to what I wanted from him.

- When riding King, I kept the arena work to short sessions, asking him to tolerate the routine, and then took him to the outdoor jumping arena or even on a trail ride to let him have fun.

After a few days of lessons with King, I began working with Heidi. This owner/horse relationship could only work out if Heidi became a confident rider on King. Riding in the arena, I had Heidi put her hands on King's withers and not direct him with her reins: she had to allow him to choose where he went and have faith in his ability to take care of her. She began at a walk; Heidi was very unsure but, after a few sessions, she found she could relax and trust him. She then began trotting. After a few more times she could maneuver King with her body, and even transition up and down from a walk to a trot and back to a walk, not using the reins.

Our next test was out on the trail. I put Heidi in the lead, then I would leap frog in front of her on my horse. In the beginning, King did not want anyone in front of him. Once Heidi became more assertive, she would circle him when he got too strong. Then allowing him to have the lead position back when he calmed down, they became a team.

On the ground, I gave Heidi a game to play to help with her confidence when leading him. He could be anywhere he wanted as long as his feet were not in front of Heidi's. If he walked in front of her, she had to give a big bump on the lead rope and make him stand still for 20 seconds, backing up if need be. Once she found she had control—and she didn't have to put up with him walking in front of her—they got along much better.

Later I learned her husband, a *Powerful*, had selected King for her. He has since become King's primary rider and Heidi has found a nice quiet mare to ride. Heidi, however, did bond with King and when she brought along a friend to ride, Heidi would ride King and put her friend on her mare.

CHAPTER 15

The Actor (RBI)

Reserved, Devoted, Intense

The *Actor* is usually a one-person horse. You must be confident and gentle, offering him the safety he needs. Once he trusts you, he will be loyal to you and do whatever you ask. The *Actor* will look to you as the herd leader, following and watching you. When he feels secure with an owner he will love being groomed, rubbed, and doted on, and he'll stand quietly awaiting your next command.

This horse likes routine and consistent work in the arena, and is very athletic and quick. He is a perfectionist when secure. He thrives when mentally and emotionally "at peace."

The *Actor* knows exactly where his feet are at all times. He is very sensitive to the human touch and body language: when you look to the right, this horse will go right. If you ask for a specific tempo, his feet will "dance" for you (fig. 15.1).

Caution

When frightened this horse has a tendency to kick out behind, so always talk to him when approaching him from the rear.

WHICH DISCIPLINE AND WHY

The *Actor* is usually good at:

- *Dressage*—He is consistent, precise and likes routine.

- *Western pleasure*—Consistent, he likes to work in the arena, goes slowly and keeps balanced.

- *Western and English equitation*—He can operate slowly, is balanced, and does exactly what he's asked to do.

- *Trail classes*—Knows where his feet are at all times and is precise.

Note: See chapter 8, p. 121, for more on the disciplines and activities suitable for the Actor.

TRAITS AND DIFFICULTIES TO CONSIDER

- Fear of disengaging the hindquarters. Instinct tells the Actor that doing so will make him vulnerable.

Actor: Character Strengths & Weaknesses	
STRENGTHS	**WEAKNESSES**
• Adaptable • Submissive • Quiet • Listens • Intense	• Distrustful • Hesitant • Timid • Fearful • Unpredictable

15.1

- Dislikes being longed. When an *Actor* doesn't trust you, he will not come in off the circle; instead he'll back up or skitter off.

- Moving forward with confidence. He needs subtle aids and a quiet voice. If you use "large" body language or are loud, this horse will be frightened.

TRAINING TIPS AND TECHNIQUES

- You must go slowly.

- Give him "dwell" time on what you are asking.

- Should this horse get overwhelmed, you must retreat, and when necessary, retreat again.

- Be gentle yet confident. Pushing too hard or fast will cause him to become unpredictable.

- Don't try to teach something new when he has his attention on something else.

- Don't ask too much at once. The *Actor* does not multitask. He is much better when you keep the lessons short and work on one new thing at a time. Then you can go back and review the work the horse knows, thus giving him self-confidence.

- When you approach an *Actor*, you must exhibit "peace." He needs safety and reassurance more than the other personality types. Go quietly to the stall door or gate and stand for a minute. Think about your body and what it is saying. Are your eyes soft? Is your voice quiet? Are you putting out a calm feeling?

- If this horse turns his tail to you or pins his ears, it's best to retreat.

Give him time to dwell on your presence. When he is ready, he will come to you. Approach and retreat as much as needed is the way to get him to learn to trust you.

- When the *Actor* is fearful, he can be a handful, sensing "things" all around and appearing to be worried over nothing. He will sweat, spin, lock up, and then explode. Don't try to force him to approach something that scares him. If you can, ask him to stop. If you must, retreat to a safe place. If he spins around, try a one-rein stop, all the time rubbing to calm him with your other hand. Once he has stopped, just let him settle. If you must get by the "fearful item," this might be a good time to dismount and be a good leader. Approach slowly, retreat if needed, and speak confidently but quietly. The *Actor* needs some time to feel safe. Once you have proved you will take care of him, he will try much harder to deal with something that frightens him.

- As an *Actor*, security is a high priority. Routine, slow and calm are security. He does not deal well with loud voices or "large" body language. When treated aggressively, he may well withdraw inward and never recover. (Following severe abuse, *Actors* are one of the hardest rescue horses to rehab.)

- When working on the longe line, the *Actor* can easily become mindless. Think of the horse that goes around and around and doesn't appear to be aware of his surroundings at all. You may have to interrupt the brain pattern to bring the horse back to you mentally. But once you do, he may be fearful about coming in off the circle. Proceed slowly with any new lessons. Give him verbal support as well as time to think about what you are asking him.

- When pushed too fast, such as on a trail ride into an unknown area, the *Actor* may "freeze" while seeing or hearing something new, then "explode." If you are attuned to him, you may recognize this tension building and go to work on calming him. This is a good time to do some lateral moves, make a circle, anything to keep him focused on *you*.

For many, the *Actor* is the hardest horse to train. Much like an oversensitive child, understanding when to coddle and when to direct is no easy task.

Remember, go slowly with the training; allow him time to ponder what you are asking him. And if he becomes scared or overwhelmed: retreat, retreat, and retreat again! Be gentle. This is the type of horse that will go much farther (and faster) when you just slow down and allow him time.

PERSONALITY PITFALLS WITH THE *ACTOR*

Human Introverts
Mediator—You are the best choice because you have the patience and kindness this horse needs. However, you may need to bring up your own confidence level to assume the leadership role.

Analyst—You will work out okay, however, you must not become mechanical; this horse likes repetition and security.

Note: A leader who lacks confidence will cause this horse to become confused and fearful.

Human Extroverts
Powerful—You will need to slow down. *Powerfuls* often want more progress in a shorter amount of time than the horse is capable of doing.

Advocate—You may be too much of a high-energy person for the *Actor* so in order to get along with him you will need to learn to quiet your emotions and your body language.

Note: An overconfident and aggressive leader will struggle to keep this horse from going emotionally "inward," or becoming dangerous because he is being made so fearful.

PUTTING IT INTO PRACTICE

Marry's Case Study: **Lilly**

Lilly, an Arabian/Quarter Horse mare, came to me as a three-year-old. When I first met her, I did a quick visual assessment and determined the following indicators of an *Actor*:

- Ears were longer and narrower than her breed standard, indicating she might be inconsistent. However, the tips were very close-set, which often indicate an *Actor*.

- Large nose with flaring nostrils, indicating she was worried and nervous, a trait often seen in right-brained horses.

- Medium to small jowl indicating she lacked confidence and would be hard to teach. This is often seen with an introverted personality.

- High-headed with eyes that showed a lot of white (right-brained).

She was also unpredictable and untrusting, traits that made her very inconsistent. True to an *Actor* nature, Lilly kicked out in the rear when under stress. She displayed the following behaviors:

- One day you would find her in the stall excited with ears up but the next day, she would be standing in the back of the stall with ears pinned back. If you didn't stop at the door, she would kick out at you.

- She could appear tense and distrustful, then quiet and obedient.

- She might seem shy then all of a sudden explode.

Before starting the training session I did the usual pain assessment and fixed the issues.

During training sessions, Lilly had problems disengaging her hindquarters, looking you in the eye and moving forward. I quickly determined that to work with this horse I would need to take on the personality of an Introvert. Sometimes I had to be a right-brain Introvert and treat the horse with lots of love and kindness. Other times I had to use my left-brain Introvert skills using more attention to detail and logical thinking.

I knew from the start that when I walked up to the stall, I had to be ready to work at her pace, not mine. I would open the door, stand and talk to her for a minute, allowing her to be the one to decide she was ready to go to work. This is an example of an Introvert behavior needed from me—an extroverted human personality would have driven her over the edge!

I gave Lilly many kind words and rubs—*not* pats or slaps on the neck—fear is already a factor with this type. I needed to be calm, quiet, relaxed and willing to give—and then give some more.

Lilly was very easy to teach to stand still, back up, and drop her head from the slightest pressure. What she struggled with was disengaging her hindquarters because when you ask the horse to do this, you are taking away her ability to bolt. Remember, the hind end contains the engine of the horse. For a horse that is fearful and not trusting like Lilly, disengaging is very scary.

Also difficult for Lilly to do: leave me and go on the longe line. Lilly preferred staying close where she felt secure. Once I accomplished getting her to go out and go around the circle, then I struggled with getting her to stop, and to look at me.

Lilly was not at all confident: she had an aversion to anything she had to step on, for example, a bridge or tarpaulin, or a surface like cement. It took me a long time to get her to accept new items around and under her feet.

But, she knew exactly where her feet were and rarely tripped. Lilly was fine walking under tree limbs or through small doorways, and only had slight problems when something touched her sides.

I put plastic bags in the arena, and ask her to sidepass. She was very sensitive and would not touch a bag with her feet. Then I put some feed in a tub in the middle of a small tarp; she left the food uneaten. If there had been another horse with her, he would have got fat, and Lilly would have starved!

It took weeks of consistent work to get her to trust me so I could ask her to step on a tarp. She finally knew it would not jump up and get her.

I used the following training tactics:

- I kept her focused and didn't ask her to do things if she wasn't looking or thinking about the lesson.

- I used a kind voice and gentle strokes. I didn't get loud or punish— just redirected her. (If you were to get frustrated with a horse like this and even think about a punishment, she would become even more distrustful—and unpredictable.

- When she was standing tied to a trailer, I would need to talk to her as I approached. She needed to hear a kind voice first. Her stress response was to kick out. She did not like loud noises or yelling children—or rough riders.

After months of going slowly, asking quietly, and being consistent, Lilly finally blossomed. Her owner, a *Mediator*, took over and when ridden with the quietest hands and slow, gentle aids, Lilly became a Western pleasure champion. She liked showing off; she went slowly in wonderful form and never looked uncomfortable or strung out. She gave her trust, and the owner could ask her to try anything, which she did with ease.

CHAPTER 16

The Talker (RBE)

Spirited, Active, Impulsive

Talkers are good for trail riding as they will lead or follow, and listen well if they have a "trusted" human. This horse likes speed. He will go as fast as he can for as long as you need. When he becomes upset, however, he is one of the hardest personalities of horse to calm down. Finding the *Talker* a balance between routine and confidence will give you a wonderful partnership. Whatever you plan to do with him will take time, focus, patience, and repetition. As Eunice will tell you about her *Talker*, if he does accidentally "dismount her," he also stops to say, "I'm sorry, and I'll wait for you to get back on." Once a *Talker* bonds, he is very loyal (fig. 16.1).

Caution

When very frightened this horse has the tendency bolt. When frustrated he will rear.

WHICH DISCIPLINE AND WHY

The *Talker* is usually good at:

- *Racing*—This is a horse with heart. He will run until he drops (literally) so be aware of this.

- *Reining*—Routine patterns and moving forward with little confusion. He has the athletic ability.

- *Contesting/gymkhana*—Fast, routine once learned, will give his all.

- *Drill team*—Fast-paced, repetitious work with other horses. It is often performed at speed.

- *Trail riding*—This type of horse needs an experienced rider because there are usually changes or unexpected things happening on the trail and the horse likes to look to a leader to keep him confident and calm. When this is accomplished, he will go all day without complaint.

- *Endurance*—With an experienced and trusted rider he will go quickly across many different terrains.

Note: See chapter 8, p. 121, for more on disciplines and activities suitable for the **Talker.**

Talker: Character Strengths & Weaknesses

STRENGTHS	WEAKNESSES
• Spirited	• Panicky
• Lively	• Over-reactive
• Demonstrative	• Edgy
• Active	• High-headed
• Intense	• Fearful
• Alert	• Hyper-alert

16.1

TRAITS AND DIFFICULTIES TO CONSIDER

- This horse's natural instinct is to only move forward. Anything else will take time and understanding for him to learn.

- He tends to "anticipate" what you want him to do. He doesn't wait for a cue but jumps ahead of you.

- Backing up. This is likely the hardest movement for him to do comfortably. His natural instinct is to "fear" going backward. Repeatedly asking for one step back and then allowing him to go forward is the best way to develop his confidence.

- Working him "on line" (12- to 14-foot lead line), and asking him to stop and face you may be a challenge. Although he can find comfort in repetitive ring work, stopping him to focus on something else will cause this horse to worry about what you are expecting him to do next.

- Moving sideways (lateral work) requires him to trust you to direct his body movements clearly. He will probably better understand and perform these types of movements when you initiate them at a trot.

- Standing still. This horse is naturally more alert than horses with the other three core personalities. Instinct tells him that standing too long in one place may be dangerous. So when you ask him to stand still, you should only ask him to "tolerate" small moments of standing, not stand all day.

TRAINING TIPS AND TECHNIQUES

- Don't expect him to do well at liberty work; he needs to "feel" you in order to be secure.

- Many times he is what is called "thin-skinned." He will not like hard grooming and scrubbing. He is usually a very clean horse on his own. I like to call him the "pretty" horse. He likes verbal rewards more than "rubs."

- Give him a job and focus him; this provides security.

- Don't try to teach him when he is afraid. The lesson now needs to be about making him feeling secure.

- If he gets really worried, you must break his focus. You may have to get bigger in your body language to get his attention. Once you have his attention, get softer and stop. You cannot "match" his energy when he gets worried. I've seen many handlers with rope burns trying to keep up.

- When really afraid, retreat; don't force him to go toward something because you might get hurt. Learn to teach this horse on his own time.

- Provide repetition and consistency; this is not the horse to leave alone in a pasture for months then expect him to ride well.

- Don't expect him to ride straight lines well without time and practice.

- Doing a job over and over gives him confidence and will lead to a horse that "listens." He does not like to make changes, so keep them small; only introduce one thing in a session, and let him get used to this before moving to the next.

- Making him stand still for long periods of time is very hard for him. Understand he needs confidence, and to move.

- Asking him to stand and look at something he fears is almost impossible. You will need to keep him moving past what he fears, then return and move past again until he can think and slow his mind. Then you can ask him to stop and experience what he is afraid of.

- The great part of this horse is he rarely does anything mean. He genuinely cares about his owner. He almost never kicks at or strikes at you. Every bad reaction is done out of fear and he is really careful to not hurt his owner when he rears. Once he gets it, he gets it, but it takes time.

- Rehabbing him is not always easy. He needs a rider who will be the decision-maker, confident and calming. When his fear is too large for him to deal with, move out and away, refocus, get the feet moving the way you want, be calm and approach again. Once you feel him breathing quietly, then you can ask him to stop and deal with the situation.

The *Talker* does best with someone who is energetic but willing to take the time necessary to gain his trust. You will need to be consistent and confident but remain calm when he gets worried. You will need to be confident enough to "ride it out" as they say because he will need to move his feet through the fear.

PERSONALITY PITFALLS WITH THE TALKER

Human Extroverts

Advocate—You will be the best match for the *Talker* because you both enjoy going anywhere and getting there quickly, but don't push too hard. This horse is often fearful and needs guidance and confidence.

Powerful—You will need to work on your patience. If this horse is fearful he will need a lot of repetitive work to help him become confident.

Note: An overly assertive leader can cause this horse to mistrust the human/horse relationship and he will work hard just to get away from the situation.

Human Introverts

Analyst—You need to understand that this horse can move very quickly and he may not think before he reacts.

Mediator—At times, you will need to bring your energy up to the horse's energy level, and when you do, you will need to become less emotional and match the horse's energy. However, your caring ways will be good for giving the horse comfort and peace.

Note: A leader who lacks confidence might affect this type negatively; the horse moves with no direction or concern for his (or your) safety.

PUTTING IT INTO PRACTICE

Marry's Case Study: **Sara**

Sara is a six-year-old Warmblood mare who had just completed 90 days with another trainer. Because Sara was still experiencing problems when she returned to her owner, Jack (an Extrovert), Jack gave me a call. On my first visit, she reared three times as he led her to the arena. She was nervous, too alert to anything that moved, white-eyed and high-headed. The following attributes lead me to believe Sara was a *Talker*:

- Long narrow forehead, an indicator of Right Brain.

- Thin-skinned with a beautiful coat, sign of an Extrovert.

- Hyper-alert, she could not focus on a task without spooking.

- High-headed, the veins in her neck looked ready to pop out.

- Over-reactive: she could not stand still because she was fearful.

- Reared: her response to the least amount of pressure—a right-brained trait.

During training sessions with Sara, she saw "monsters" in trees everywhere she went. Anything new created a flight response. If she couldn't bolt forward, she went up.

Doing a physical assessment I found no pain. Later, I found her saddle did not fit well, which had been adding to her distress. Sara was very concerned about anything new so it took quite a few saddle changes to find one she was comfortable with on her back. Once we found the right saddle, Sara worked much harder to settle into the lesson.

I always start training with groundwork. I believe if you can't get it done nicely from the ground, it's not going to be much prettier or easier from the saddle.

During training sessions I worked with getting her to drop her head and relax her jaw by putting my finger in the bit seat of her mouth to cause chewing. Then I asked her for flexions, which allowed her a place of comfort and helped her to "stand." Backing up was very hard for her. She would lock up and when you pushed a bit more, she would rear. We had to take it very slowly, one step at a time. Because of her rearing I chose not to teach her the wiggle back in the beginning, instead using thumb pressure on her chest to ask for the back. This is her heart area, and also a place of comfort for a more right-brained horse.

Working through desensitizing was an ongoing issue with her. Just tossing a rope over her back was not going to happen easily. She would jump sideways or bolt forward. I was pretty sure someone had inappropriately used a rope or whip before. I began by just rubbing the rope up and down and asking her to relax. Then I lightly tapped her with the rope, and alternated between tapping and rubbing. It took many sessions to be able to toss a rope over her back and have her stay calm—not fearfully trying to run away.

When I was ready to start longeing and asked her to go forward, she would jump and try to run around me, stop and stand white-eyed in fear, then try to run off again. She could not walk off quietly.

I had to work at longeing in baby steps. I would put her along the wall of the arena, take one step back, make a kissing noise and she was off! There was no problem having her run forward, but it took many times of repeating this process to get her to walk. The wonderful part was once she did find her self-confidence, she transitioned up and down and easily turned on her haunches. She was extremely light and soft.

In another longeing lesson for Sara, I set up four cavalletti poles to keep her focused with her feet moving. Sara was afraid to even think about stopping to look at the pole. She would rush right through them never tipping one over. She knew exactly where her feet were at all times—one of the wonderful traits of the more right-brained horses. I had to ask her to stop a few feet in front of the pole and again "drop her head" and remain calm. Once she was walking calmly through the poles, we began trotting through them, which she did impressively. However, if she did happen to hit one, it would totally send her into a panic, causing her to speed up or jump sideways out of the line of poles.

As we progressed into riding, I found I had trouble teaching Sara how to sidepass. My usual way of teaching a sidepass is to have Sara face a wall, then by using my leg and rein aids, ask her to take a step over sideways. Being a *Talker* she had to learn while her feet were moving so I taught her to first half-pass down the rail.

It took some time before we could open a gate. Asking her to first stop her feet and relax and second, to sidepass over to open it was difficult for her. She was very worried about bumping her sides on the gate.

The great advantage to *Talkers* is they typically are very athletic; they know where to put their feet and instinctively know how to take care of themselves. Once Sara learned to trust people and handle her fears by allowing her rider to be the leader, she could be ridden anywhere for as long as the rider wanted to ride. Sara and Jack (also an *RBE*) ended up doing well in endurance.

CHAPTER 17

The "Rescue" Horse
and Other Training Tips

Rehabilitating the Abused Horse

This chapter is intended to help those of you who have decided to try rehabilitating an abused horse. It is a noble effort, and we applaud you. However, even with the best of intentions, the rescuer can sometimes be very hard on such a horse. So if you take on a "rescue" horse, be sure to read this carefully.

First, you must understand your personality style so you can determine whether you will be the best possible handler for an already stressed horse. Remember, if you have an extreme core personality (very high score) it will be hard for you to align to the changing personality needs of an abused horse and most rescue horses need plenty of patience and understanding.

Next, if possible you should try to determine the horse's core personality *before* the abuse occurred so you can help him get back to a comfortable and safe place. Sometimes you are able to talk with previous owners, other times you have to make your best judgment as a result of how the horse reacts *most* of the time. It's not always easy because a horse that has been stressed or starved is living on the instinct of fear. It can be hard to determine if he is more *flight* reactive (right-brained) or more *fight* reactive (left-brained).

When placed with a "mismatched" human, an abused horse can become so withdrawn, he becomes completely unresponsive. Even worse, this horse may become so mean, he can no longer be trusted or be safely used for any purpose.

Sadly, some people use horrific "training" methods on their horses. This was the case with a horse I once owned. The owner sent him (at two years old) to a "trainer" that tied him to a barn wall and "beat him into submission." This was an extroverted horse and the trainer was convinced he had to learn to stand still.

After this terrible treatment, the horse went through six owners in seven years. By the time I got him, he was herd bound and already dangerous: on the ground, if you raised your hand next to his head he would attempt to bite; and when you tried to get his attention and shake the lead rope, he would strike out at you with his front feet. When riding, and you tried to turn him, he would spin and bolt, or stop and try to back up rapidly.

As you can see, he displayed the core traits of several different Social Styles. In the chapter about the human personality, we described the "Z" pattern, which occurs when people are under stress (p. 15). Horses also go through several personalities in an attempt to cope with what has been inflicted upon them. (Fortunately, once I had rehabbed this horse the new owner clicked with him and was able to bond and they had a very enjoyable partnership. He is now a wonderful horse for her, but it took years.)

So how do you train the rescued horse?

The Pain Body Evaluation comes first (see p. 167). It is even more important with a horse that has been abused. This cannot be emphasized enough. Probably 80 percent of the horses that have behavioral problems stem from pain and discomfort. Once it is determined there are no pain issues, check saddle fit, teeth, and feet. Only then, should you start rehabilitation and training.

As mentioned above, the horse may stress through multiple personalities. Over time, however, most rescue horses can go back to being emotionally balanced. Unfortunately, some do not.

As with any good training program there are some common first steps:

- Do a pain evaluation (see above and p. 167).

- Observe and know a horse's conformation to be sure he can do what you are asking.

- Understand the stress response of each core personality. Learn to observe. How does the horse act in a stall, out in a pasture with herd mates, when he sees a human approach?

- Go to the stall door and wait. What kind of reaction do you get? Does the horse look interested in you, or want to be left alone? Is he alert or does he appear depressed? Think about your body language: how would the horse be "reading" you?

- Wait for him to make eye contact with you. Don't think you can just walk right in, join up with him and be friends.

- Learn his body language. Is he acting as if he is fearful? Does he want to trust or is he just tuning out as much as he can?

- Get to know him. Take as much time as he needs. Don't try to rush him to be what you want him to be.

- Don't start any training until he shows you he is ready. The longest way is many times the shortest way. Timing is everything.

It is important to give him time and opportunity to develop a sense of security. If you have a small area where you can just be with him, take a stool and a book and sit there reading until he comes up to you. A curious horse is a horse building up self-confidence. Watch for this before you begin any training sessions.

Marry's Case Study: **Pegasus**

Here is an example of an abused *Thinker* that had stressed to an *Actor*.

Pegasus is an Arabian rescued at 10 years old. He has had six different owners in his life. Some were very caring, while others were very abusive.

When I first met Pegasus he would pin his ears and only allow certain people to touch him. He could read a person's intentions and was very cautious about letting any aggressive person get near him. I found he was in a lot of physical pain. He had 22 vertebrae out in his spine. His neck was misaligned so badly he had been rubbing it hard on posts trying to fix it. This caused open wounds to appear on his neck.

I called an equine chiropractor and a massage therapist to work on him. It was approximately eight visits and six months later before he was physically ready for the next step in rehabilitation.

Prior to this time, Pegasus would react to fear by kicking or bolting—the *Actor*'s reaction to stress—but most of the time I observed him he acted much more like a *Thinker*. He could be pushy, getting in your personal space when wanting attention; he enjoyed playing ground games in the pasture and was relaxed with the other horses in the herd. To begin repairing his emotional state, for the first 10 days I applied an herbal relaxer (Rescue Remedy in this case, but there are others) to his feed. I would hold the bucket while he ate, talking quietly and allowing him to relax. This taught him to trust me as *Thinkers* do like their food!

As he began looking forward to our chats at dinner time, I used this time to begin other tasks such as grooming and picking out his feet. As he became curious and began to trust me, it was time to begin groundwork.

I started by working him for 15 minutes, only asking him for a few minutes more each day. I kept the lessons short and only stretched them out when he was calm. I used carrots at first, because a *Thinker* will be more willing to "try" if he is rewarded with a treat.

Anytime he showed signs of nervousness, such as pinning his ears, or moving away quickly, I asked him to handle a task that was easier for him, such as standing and dropping his head. I waited for him to lick and chew showing that once again he was relaxed and ready to move on. At this point, I would reward him and call it a day. (Never stop a session with a behavior you don't want to live with when working with any horse, but especially with a *Thinker*.)

Thinkers do get bored easily. But it was because he had been abused that I kept the sessions short: he was only capable of coping with small changes at a time.

Once his groundwork was solid I found he was on the more extroverted side of being a *Thinker* than normal. He did have energy and I'm sure some of this could be attributed to his being an Arabian. But the fact was that he loved to stand and be groomed, which is much more of an Introvert then Extrovert trait.

Desensitizing took much longer then it would for a normal *Thinker*, who is generally curious. He was very worried about stepping on obstacles like a tarp (right-brained trait), but once he was over his fear, he found them entertaining. He began picking up the tarp with his mouth and dragging it around (left-brained trait).

I leave hula hoops in the pasture to help the horses deal with stepping on things that make noise, along with them being able to be used as toys. He was frightened of them at first, and had he been a *core* right-brained horse he would have kept avoiding them. But being a left-brained horse, he got over that fear and now plays with the hoops so hard they are always broken.

We had some issues with the farrier, a wonderful lady who is a *Powerful*-type personality. I had thought he was fine with his feet but when she was holding one up and he tried to pull it out of her hand (left-brained trait) she was loud in her verbal commands to stop. He jumped forward, spun and kicked her (*Actor* trait). As she was rubbing her leg, Pegasus ran from the barn but quickly returned putting his head down as if apologizing for his actions. Although still nervous, he did stand for the other three feet to be trimmed. This was another sign that he was a *Thinker*.

Had he been a truly right-brained horse, he would have gone off and not had any thought of returning. Even when caught, a right-brained horse would have "mentally" been finished for the day and need more work on handling his feet before a return visit from the farrier.

In the year I have been with Pegasus, most days he is curious and confident. He likes moving forward and has no problem going for long rides. Now when Pegasus does become concerned, his core personality comes out. He stops, may even lower his head and snort, but his feet stay planted, and once he understands the threat is not something that will get him, he will let out a large breath and be ready to move forward again.

The problems that I am still working on 18 months later are ones that manifested from emotional stress. His physical self is 95 percent healed. His emotional state is only about 60 percent healed.

At this time the saddle work is still in the arena for the most part (longer than I would normally work a *Thinker* there). Once he is confident and appears to be getting bored with it, we will be ready to go out on the trails. My belief is that given enough time and careful training (understanding his past and what stresses him) he will become a wonderful mount.

I enjoy working with rescue horses, I don't expect them to change overnight and some are simply horses that are what I fondly call "project" horses. I have no time limit on when they will be healed. As long as they are not in physical pain or mentally without possibility of being healed, I don't worry about how fast they will come around.

Pegasus' *Thinker* Traits:
- Curious.
- Pushy with pasture mate.
- Food-oriented.
- Can dominate.
- Bored easily.
- Confident—most of the time.
- Unconcerned—most of the time.

Human Personality Reactions to Pegasus

Analysts—Are willing to take the time to work through Pegasus' concerns.

Powerfuls—Have the confidence Pegasus needs for a rider but will need to ride with less aggression. You will need to learn this horse thrives on reward, both verbal and food.

Advocates—Are probably the hardest riders on this horse. They want a horse that is happy to run through the fields or work all day. They often use more aggressive aids, which might be too much for Pegasus. When you push this horse too fast and for too long you will stress him. You need to ride more quietly and have fewer expectations for how long and hard he can work.

Mediators—They will have to show their confident side or this horse might test them for the leadership. Pegasus will find security from your quiet body movements. You're fine with letting him stop and think about something worrying him, but you must be sure to tell him "It's okay, now let's move on."

Note: Adopting a rescue horse can be most rewarding. Many of these horses are so happy to be fed and cared for they have no problems adjusting to a new home. Unfortunately with some extremely abused horses this is not the case, and dealing with such cases is not for the faint of heart. You must be willing to observe the horse in all situations to find out his "core" personality and then train him accordingly.

Training Methods Summary: *Do's*

THINKER	WORKER	ACTOR	TALKER
Have a purpose. (Hates repetition—gets dull.)	Introduce new lessons. (Gets bored easily—is naughty.)	Go slowly. Retreat if necessary. (Reacts to aggressive methods.)	Keep focused on the job. (Becomes unfocused easily.)
Be very clear what you are asking. (Will take advantage if you don't.)	Make many transitions to different gaits. (Reacts to being bored.)	Be gentle. Use quiet hands. Do not "pat," rub instead. (Gets nervous with "big" body language and movement.)	Interrupt pattern if horse gets worried. (Runs you in circles.)
Use treats and "love" to your advantage. (Responds well.)	Keep moving and change direction. Teach through fun. (Responds well to new things.)	Use quiet voice and body language. (Responds well to slow and quiet.)	Use repetition, provide consistent work. (Finds comfort in routine.)
		When longeing keep him focused. Maintain steady speed.	When longeing change direction when focus is lost. Be clear about speed.

12.3

A Few Trainers' Tricks

Everyone can benefit from a few tricks used by good trainers. Next time you are with your horse—or meeting a new one for the first time—try these ideas:

- When you are nervous chew gum (be sure you can walk and chew gum at the same time!) The chewing motion is something the horse will understand as a sign of relaxation.

Training Methods Summary: *Dont's*

THINKER	WORKER	ACTOR	TALKER
"Make" him work: "Convince" him instead.	Punish for disobedience: Keep going and stay focused.	Ask for too much in one session: Provide many "mental" breaks.	Ask him to do precise work.
Do too many circles.	"Make" him go too slowly.	Use loud voice or large body language.	Ask him to stop his feet when fearful.
Keep him at one speed.	Bore him.	Ask him to do anything when fearful and unfocused.	Work on straight lines for too long and "mentally" stress him.
When longeing, don't stand in one place too long. Change speeds.	Don't work on a longe line that is too short or too long. Boredom sets in.		

12.4

- Whether you are putting on a halter or a bridle, learn to stand at the shoulder and ask your horse to bend his head back to you. Don't force him, but wait for him to comply. This keeps you in a safe position, and teaches your horse to trust and respect you as his leader.

- Blow in your horse's nose. It is his way of communicating and saying hello.

- Eat an apple or a mint before meeting him. Yes, even horses like nice smelling breath!

- When working from the ground and your horse becomes over-alert, high-headed, or is not focusing on you, try putting your finger (know a horse's mouth first, please) inside the bit "seat" and rub the gums. This gets him to open and release his jaw, allowing him to "chew" and relax.

- Learn that an open or light hand is an open heart to a horse. He does not learn by the pressure you apply, he learns by the release you give him when he tries.

- Teach your horse to lower his head. There are two ways to achieve this: from pressure on the lead rope or by putting slight hand pressure halfway down the neck on his mane. 1) Begin with slight pressure on the lead rope, releasing for the slightest try. When you are leading a horse and he becomes nervous ask him to lower his head to relax: a horse with a lowered head shows relaxation and trust—plus he enjoys stretching his topline. 2) When you are riding and your horse gets nervous, you can put your hand on his neck and tell him to drop his head and he will find comfort.

- Practice mounting your horse from both sides while you are standing on a car bumper, trailer, or stump. You never know when you won't have a mounting block handy. If your horse won't stand still at any of these places, be sure he is not reacting to pain (or your toe jabbing his side).

- When you feel your horse becoming nervous try leaning back and rubbing him on the rump. By leaning back just that slight amount, you are repositioned to a place he will feel that you are relaxed. (Be sure you have desensitized him to having a hand touch his rump.)

- Be aware of a swishing tail, a head bobbing up and down, or a horse that appears to be asleep. Everything a horse does will have a meaning. Learn to be observant, learn to listen. Every moment you spend with a horse is a training session. You are either asking him to allow you to be the leader, or he is giving you feedback on whether you are a good or bad leader. When with your horse you are in a herd of two.

- When it comes to horses, less is always more. As mentioned, if a horse can feel a fly land on his mane, he can also feel your hand at the end of the lead rope or longe line. Keep your hands light on the rein or lead, thus allowing him to feel when you squeeze then wait for your next request.

Conclusion

WE HOPE WE have in some small way helped you find and "create" your perfect equine partner. If we also helped you with a person or two along the way, that's even better. Most of all, we hope we have opened your eyes to the fact that not all horse problems are training issues; pain is often overlooked as a factor. Give your horse the benefit of the doubt. Check his back, teeth, feet, muscles, and nerves, and be sure his saddle and bridle fit before you begin riding or training. Understand it's okay to sell a horse that doesn't fit your needs and find one that does because there truly are horses and riders that just don't match.

We would like you to understand that you—and only you—can know what you need in a horse. Consider the following guidelines:

Understand what kind of person you are. Deciding on whether you are Introvert or Extrovert is the primary basis for your selection of the horse. After that, your confidence level is the deciding factor.

- Decide which discipline you would like to pursue.

- Research the breed of horse to find one best suited for your desired activity.

- Work to find the horse that best suits your needs.

- Make multiple trips to the horse's current home. Find out if his personality truly matches yours. If not, is it a horse you love so much that you are willing to change your personality until you both find a perfect balance? Ask yourself whether you can live with that horse when he is under stress.

- Fall in love with this horse and learn to give with your heart (sometimes not an easy task for the logic-based owner).

Good luck in your quest to "know you and know your horse" and choose the right horse for you.

Take a deep breath and enjoy the journey!

About the Authors

Meet Eunice

Hi, I'm Eunice. I'm responsible for the "human side" of this book. I have a degree in Business and Math from Indiana University and a Masters of Science in Information Technology from Ball State. And no, I can't program my cell phone, GPS, or laptop, and yes, my DVD player flashes 12:00.

I have spent the past 25-plus years in management, sales, and adult education, including owning my own business. One of the things I enjoyed most about my many jobs was the opportunity to teach others how to be good salespeople—I did this by teaching employees how to read personality traits and align their own personality appropriately with clients. To do this successfully, I spent a large amount of time studying exactly what makes people "tick," and how to manage them, sell to them, educate them, and form partnerships with them.

Please note: the degrees I earned did not directly relate to the study of psychology. Everything I know and present in this book comes from practical work experience and my own personal research. Most of the information on human personalities is not new. I've just put what I've learned from others over the years in one place.

In my spare time, I have always ridden horses. I currently own three, as well as a donkey. I am a *Powerful*. Bo, my 32-year-old and long-time friend, is a *Worker*. He is a Tennessee Walker and very much an "all go, take you anywhere safely" kind of horse. Dakota, my 17-year-old Quarter/Draft cross, is a *Thinker*. He is very lazy and I only use him for trick horse performances—he's perfect for that. Joker, a Mountain Pleasure Horse and my current "best bud," is very much a *Talker*. We have shared many trails in many states, at speed of course, over the past four years. Barney the donkey is a rescue project; he is just my "watch dog" right now.

Eunice and her Mountain Pleasure Horse Joker.

Meet Marry

Hello, I'm Marry. I'm responsible for the "horse side" of this book. I began riding at age seven, and in the years that followed was an active trail rider as well as competitor. I have shown English, Western, and saddle seat; I've jumped, done competitive trail, and explored dressage. At age 17, I was introduced to the world of natural horsemanship and studied many clinicians before meeting Frank Bell and becoming one of his certified trainers.

Now I spend my time giving natural horsemanship clinics and teaching lessons. I help clients train their own horses, and I work with equine rescue groups to rehabilitate abused horses for new homes.

Helping to connect horse and owner in a way that forms a partnership built on confidence, leadership, and love is my passion. I am an *Analyst* and I own two horses that are *Thinkers*. One is a foundation Quarter Horse that is very much on the "lazy" side of the *Thinker* personality and the other is an Arabian that is far more clever and quick!

Marry and her two horses.

Acknowledgments

WE WANT TO THANK everyone who contributed to our research. Many people willingly took the questionnaires we gave, while others spent hours allowing us to interview them. Some proofread and others contributed expertise in one area or another. You were all wonderful for sharing your time with us and helping to confirm our theories.

A special thanks goes to Carla Waechter for her input and Sharon Moseley for her endless work on the manuscript.

We also want to thank Trafalgar Square Books, and especially Caroline Robbins who spent countless hours editing. Finding a format that is easy to read and entertaining while still educational is not an easy task.

A very big thank you goes to Judy Masters for her input on the Social Styles and related materials, as well as to the breeders who so generously gave of their time.

We have learned so much: None of this would have been possible without each of you.

Index